Legal Issues in the Private Practice of Psychiatry

THE PRIVATE PRACTICE MONOGRAPH SERIES

Sponsored by

The American Psychiatric Association
Committee on Private Practice
and
Committee on Special Benefit Programs

SPRING 1984

Computers and Other Technological Aids for Psychiatric Private Practice
Jonathan D. *Lieff,* M.D.

Legal Issues in the Private Practice of Psychiatry
Joel I. *Klein, JoAnn* E. *Macbeth, and Joseph* N. *Onek*

Personal and Business Tax and Financial Planning for Psychiatrists
W. *Murray Bradford,* C.P.A., *and Glenn* B. *Davis,* J.D., LL.M. *(Tax)*

FALL 1984

Establishing a Psychiatric Private Practice
Linda Logsdon, M.D.

Winding Down a Psychiatric Private Practice
Joseph Deacon, J.D.

Legal Issues in the Private Practice of Psychiatry

by
Joel I. Klein
JoAnn E. Macbeth
Joseph N. Onek

Onek, Klein & Farr
Washington, D.C.

1400 K Street, N.W.
Washington, D.C. 20005

Copyright © 1984 by Onek, Klein & Farr
Printed in the United States of America

Library of Congress Cataloging in Publication Data

Klein, Joel I.
    Legal issues in the private practice of psychiatry.

    (The Private practice monograph series)
    Bibliography: p. 76
    1. Psychiatrists—Malpractice—United States.
2. Confidential communications—Physicians—United States.
3. Psychiatrists—Legal status, laws, etc.—United States.
I. Macbeth, JoAnn E. II. Onek, Joseph. III. Title. IV. Series
[DNLM: 1. Psychiatry—United States—legislation.
WM   33   AA1   K6L]
KF2910.P753.K58   1984   346.7303'32   84-6506
ISBN 0-88048-101-3   (soft)   347.306332

Contents

About the Authors   *viii*

Preface   *ix*

Introduction   *x*

1 Malpractice   2

Liability for Emotional Injury Due to Negligent Psychotherapy   4

    Electroconvulsive Therapy   5

    Sexual Therapy and Sexual Relationships with Patients   5

    Drug Treatment   7

Liability for Abandonment: Creation and Termination of the Physician-Patient Relationship   11

Liability for Patients' Acts of Violence   13

Liability for Patient Suicides   19

    Suicide by Hospitalized Patients   20

    Suicide Following Discharge from a Hospital   21

    Suicide by Outpatients   22

    Reducing the Risk of Liability   23

Consent to Treatment   24

    Informed Consent   24

    Consent in General Medical and Outpatient Psychiatric Contexts: Competency and Substituted Consent   27

Liability Arising from Employer, Supervisory, and Consultative Relationships   29

    Employer Relationships   29

    Supervisory Relationships   29

    Consultative Relationships   30

2 Confidentiality and Privilege   32

Physician-Patient and Psychotherapist-Patient Privilege   33

    Coverage of Statutes   33

    Waiver of the Privilege   34

    Exceptions to the Privilege   35

    Determining Whether Privilege Applies   37

Responding to a Subpoena   37
Psychiatrists' Duty of Confidentiality   39
Other Risks of Breaching Confidentiality   42
Confidentiality after a Patient's Death   43
Confidentiality and Minor Patients   44
   Young Minors   45
   Adolescents   46
Confidentiality and Authorization to Release
   Information   47

3 Psychiatric Records   50
Maintaining Records   53
Keeping Records Confidential   54
Patient Access to Records   55

4 Billing and Payment Issues   56
Limitations on Collection Methods   58
Facilitating Collection   59
Billing for Missed Sessions and Treatment-Related
   Services   59
Charging Interest   60

Notes   62
Appendix 1: Additional Readings   76
Appendix 2: Model Forms   78
Consent for Treatment   79
Termination of Psychiatrist-Patient Relationship   80
Patient Authorization for Release of Medical
   Information   81
Agreement to Pay for Treatment of Relative   82
**Appendix 3: The Principles of Medical Ethics with
Annotations Especially Applicable to Psychiatry   84**

About the Authors

Joel I. Klein received his law degree magna cum laude from Harvard University, where he served as Articles Editor for the Harvard Law Review. Mr. Klein also holds a degree from Columbia College. Mr. Klein, who was admitted to the bar in 1973, is presently General Counsel to the American Psychiatric Association.

JoAnn E. Macbeth received her law degree from Columbia University and was admitted to the bar in 1976. Ms. Macbeth also holds a degree from Wellesley College.

Joseph N. Onek received his law degree magna cum laude from Yale Law School, where he served as Note and Comment Editor of the Yale Law Journal. Mr. Onek also holds degrees from Harvard University and the London School of Economics and was admitted to the bar in 1968.

Preface

The authors wish to thank the American Psychiatric Association's Committee on Private Practice, chaired by Naomi Goldstein, M.D., for proposing the preparation of this monograph. They also wish to thank Dr. Goldstein for her thoughtful comments on the manuscript.

The authors were assisted in preparing this manuscript by their colleagues at Onek, Klein & Farr. The authors emphasize that, although their firm serves as general counsel to the American Psychiatric Association, this monograph represents the views of the authors and not necessarily those of the Association.

Finally, it is important to point out that, while this monograph seeks to highlight significant legal issues, set out discernible trends, and provide general guidance, it is not a substitute for legal representation. Likewise, although psychiatrists need to be mindful of the legal issues that affect their practice, there is an unfortunate tendency among some to view the law as a brooding omnipresence, requiring the practice of defensive, if not bad, medicine. The authors hope that this monograph will help psychiatrists in negotiating the legal minefield, without encouraging a defensive posture. In the end, patients need good psychiatrists. Even today legal advice is not a recognized form of treatment for mental illness.

Introduction

Today the practice of psychiatry is permeated by the law. By statute, regulation, and decision, the legislatures, administrators, and courts have limited the psychiatrist's freedom in making treatment decisions, affected the levels and mechanisms of compensation, and curtailed his discretion to release information. The threat of law suits and the specter of large damage awards are now a common part of a psychiatrist's professional life (1).

The increase in litigation is in part the product of new theories, and has opened up new areas of liability. Ten years ago psychiatrists were undoubtedly concerned about the medical and social implications for patients placed on antipsychotics that might cause tardive dyskinesia and for patients who threatened third parties. Today, it is the rare psychiatrist who is not equally concerned about the potential for suit in such situations. Even more alarming, the new legal obligations on psychiatrists sometimes seem to be in conflict with one another. At the same time that the law is imposing greater liability for breaches of confidentiality, it may also require that the psychiatrist violate traditional concepts of confidentiality by warning a third party that a patient has threatened to harm him.

Basic understanding of the law affecting psychiatric practice is essential to competent professional handling of patients. Uncertainty and anxiety about the law and the responsibilities and obligations it imposes are detrimental to effective treatment and may result in a reluctance to treat certain patients. This monograph attempts to dispel some of the uncertainty by identifying the most serious risks for the private practitioner and by suggesting ways of minimizing risks and a framework within which to analyze conflicting duties. It does not resolve all ambiguities or point the way to risk-free psychiatry: Like medicine, the law is uncertain and frequently in a state of flux. In addition, and of great significance for readers of this monograph, legal requirements are not identical in every state. While the discussion that follows seeks to describe general legal requirements as well as trends in the law, the requirements in a particular state are, in the end, the only reliable guide for a psychiatrist who faces a specific problem or concern.

Legal Issues in the Private Practice of Psychiatry

1

Malpractice

The increase in malpractice claims against psychiatrists should be kept in perspective. The incidence of claims against psychiatrists is still much lower than against other physicians (2), and most threatened claims do not result in judgments against the psychiatrist. In one recent study of such claims, only 25 percent involved any legal process—19 percent were settled and 6 percent were adjudicated (3). These figures are a reflection of both malpractice law and the nature of psychiatric treatment and practice.

Medical malpractice consists of an act or omission by a physician acting in his or her professional capacity that results from a failure to exercise the degree of care, knowledge, and skill ordinarily possessed and exercised in similar situations by a member of the profession practicing in the same field, causing or aggravating an injury to the patient. In order to prevail in a malpractice action, a plaintiff must establish four elements by a preponderance of the evidence: 1) that the physician has assumed a duty to care for the patient; 2) that the physician has breached the duty by an act or omission not in accord with the standards of the profession; 3) that the patient was harmed; and 4) that the physician's breach of duty was the proximate cause of the harm to the patient.

A physician has no duty to a person—and there is no potential for malpractice liability—unless there is a physician–patient relationship. The existence of the relationship and duty is not questioned in most malpractice cases, but it can be the major issue when the patient charges abandonment or bases a legal action on alleged negligence in a situation in which the psychiatrist feels there was no treatment relationship with the patient. These problems should not be difficult to handle; they are discussed briefly below.

To satisfy the second element in a malpractice case—breach of duty—the plaintiff must establish a standard of care and the physician's deviation from that standard (4). This has sometimes been difficult in a psychiatric malpractice case, but is becoming easier as psychiatry becomes more established in terms of medical and scientific precision. Outside the area of psychoses, diagnosis of mental disorders is still somewhat imprecise and there are many possible methods of treatment that are recognized. In view of these considerations, courts are sometimes reluctant to find a physician negligent for following one method if it is approved by at least a respectable minority of the profession. An additional problem is that experts, whose testimony is generally necessary for this purpose, may be reluctant to testify against their colleagues. This problem, too, however, may be more reminiscent of a bygone era.

No matter how clear a psychiatrist's deviation from a standard of care, he or she will not be liable unless the patient suffered some harm. Establishing damage can be a problem for a plaintiff suing a psychiatrist. While the harm may sometimes be physical (the result of medication, ECT, inadequate supervision, etc.), what is often alleged is aggravation of a pre-existing emotional disorder. The law has been slow to compensate for purely emotional injuries. Citing the difficulty of measurement and the possibility of fictitious claims, courts only recently have begun to provide compensation for even the intentional infliction of emotional distress and still require that the defendant's conduct be outrageous. Recovery for the negligent infliction of emotional distress—the allegation in most malpractice actions—is even more difficult. Compensation is generally provided only if the mental or emotional distress is accompanied by physical harm (5).

Proximate cause, the last element in a malpractice case, can also be a problem for the plaintiff suing a psychiatrist. Knowledge of psychiatric causation is to some extent limited. In addition, the course of many disorders is not clear, making it difficult to determine if the harm is part of the natural progression of the disorder or is related to the treatment. As a consequence, most successful suits involve a claim of physical injury to the patient or a third party.

The sections below will cover the main areas of psychiatric malpractice. Discussed first will be liability for various kinds of negligent treatment and for abandonment or nonattendance. Next, liability for patients who commit suicide or harm others will be covered. Finally, a number of consent issues will be discussed.

LIABILITY FOR EMOTIONAL INJURY DUE TO NEGLIGENT PSYCHOTHERAPY

Suits for emotional injury due to negligent psychotherapy are unlikely to succeed. The general problems discussed above (which are faced by a plaintiff in any psychiatric malpractice case) are particularly acute in such suits. As a result, there are virtually no reported cases imposing liability for negligent psychotherapy resulting in purely emotional harm (6).

Psychiatrists who are concerned about the possibility of such suits frequently ask about the advisability of using consent forms for psychotherapy. It is unlikely that such a form serves any real purpose: By signing it a patient does not consent to negligent treatment but only to the effects of the treatment properly administered. On the other hand, psychotherapists often report that patients who have undergone a lengthy course of psychotherapy and then switched to another form of therapy which they feel has had dramatic results express anger and threaten suit. It may, therefore, be advisable to discuss with the patient at the outset of treatment that although the psychiatrist believes psychotherapy is indicated, there are alternative methods of treatment that the patient may want to consider and discuss with other therapists. This concern is particularly important when medication might appear appropriate but the psychiatrist believes that psychotherapy without medication is indicated. In such circumstances, a consent form, stating that the patient has been advised of other treatments but prefers psychotherapy, might then be in order.

Electroconvulsive Therapy

Traditionally, suits by patients who suffered physical injuries as a result of electroconvulsive therapy (ECT) have been common. These cases most often allege one of the following: insufficient pretreatment examination (7), negligent administration of the relaxant given before ECT, negligent administration of the therapy itself, and inadequate supervision of the patient during the period of disorientation following treatment (8). Although patients who suffer fractures, cardiac arrest, or other serious injuries are likely to sue, these injuries alone will not result in liability for the psychiatrist since they may result even when the entire process is conducted properly. Liability depends on the patient's ability to show that the psychiatrist failed to conform to standard practice in the use of ECT.

Many ECT cases are based on the doctrine of informed consent, which is discussed at greater length below. A psychiatrist sued under this doctrine who did not obtain proper consent may be liable for injuries even if the use of ECT was entirely proper. Indeed, even if there were no side effects, the psychiatrist may be liable for negligently providing inadequate disclosure, or even for assault and battery. To avoid this risk, as part of the process of obtaining consent, the psychiatrist should explain the patient's diagnosis and prognosis, the likely risks and benefits of ECT and of alternative forms of treatment. The psychiatrist should be careful not to guarantee a cure or to minimize the risks involved. If a patient has been declared legally incompetent or simply appears incapable of understanding the procedure, it may be necessary to get consent by a guardian or, more likely, to get a court order authorizing the treatment.

Sexual Therapy and Sexual Relationships with Patients

Virtually all psychiatrists believe that sexual involvement with a patient is inappropriate and undesirable (9). There is evidence of serious emotional harm and inability to benefit from subsequent therapy among patients who have had sexual relationships with their therapists (10). The American Psychiatric Association's ethical standards are unequivocal: Sexual involvement with a patient is always unethical (11).

Facing such virtually unanimous professional opinion, a psychiatrist who is shown to have had sexual contact with a patient is unlikely to escape malpractice liability (12). A recent review of malpractice suits against psychotherapists bears this out, concluding that a patient basing a suit on a psychotherapist's sexual conduct has the greatest likelihood of success (13).

To date, in every malpractice case in which a psychiatrist's sexual relationship with a patient has been established, the psychiatrist has been found liable (14). The defenses raised regularly by defendants in these cases have not met with success. Courts routinely reject the claim that the relationship was consensual, either finding that the patient's transference and involvement with the therapist precluded a truly voluntary consent or concluding that a patient cannot consent to a professionally unacceptable form of treatment. The argument that the sexual activity was part of the treatment and believed to be therapeutic by the psychiatrist has been similarly unsuccessful (15).

Psychiatrists sometimes claim that they have not committed malpractice because their sexual relationship with a patient was entirely separate from their treatment relationship. This claim would seem to have greatest force when the sexual relationship began after the end of therapy. It is by no means clear, however, that this position would protect a psychiatrist in a malpractice case (16), particularly when the sexual involvement follows soon after the termination of treatment. In addition, it is clear that termination of treatment is far from a complete defense to ethical charges. In response to an inquiry as to whether it is ethical for a psychiatrist to begin a sexual relationship with a former patient a few weeks after the termination of treatment, an ethical opinion by the APA Ethics Committee provides in part:

> Sexual activity with a patient is unethical. . . . The psychiatrist is exploiting his patient by not helping him or her to see that his or her affection for him is a projection of feelings appropriate to another person at another

point in time. Is the exploitation any less "a few weeks after terminating treatment"? A few months? A few years? The District Branch ethics committee's investigation should be able to settle the issue not simply on the basis of the time span, but on the basis of the committee's determination of the extent to which this was exploitation of the therapeutic relationship (17).

Drug Treatment

Malpractice cases based on a psychiatrist's use of psychoactive medications have been relatively infrequent considering the dramatic increase in the use of such treatment over the past two decades. However, such suits are becoming more common (18). Indeed, a study of claims filed between 1972 and 1983 against psychiatrists insured by the professional liability insurance program sponsored by the APA showed that 20 percent of the claims involved drug reactions (19).

Like other physicians, a psychiatrist who uses medication faces two kinds of legal challenges: The first, that of failure to get the informed consent of the patient or a substitute decision maker and second, that of negligence in prescribing or carrying out treatment with the drug.

Informed consent and drug treatment. Like the psychiarist who treats with electroconvulsive therapy, the psychiatrist who uses drug treatment will be risking liability if he or she proceeds without the patient's informed consent. In order for consent to treatment to be informed, the patient must be told of the diagnosis, the benefits and risks of the therapy (including the possibility of harmful side effects), alternative forms of treatment, and the likely results of receiving and not receiving the treatment. As will be discussed below, there are situations in which the requirement is relaxed and situations where the consent of someone other than the patient will need to be obtained.

Negligent prescription or administration of medications. A number of different allegations may be made in a negligent medication case. Plaintiffs frequently argue that they suffered physical injury because the psychiatrist administered a drug in a situation where its use was inappropriate, or exceeded the proper dosage although the drug was appropriate (20). Concerned about this possibility, psychiatrists frequently ask whether it is "safe" to prescribe a particular medication in a particular situation. There is limited case law specifically addressing whether use of a drug under a particular set of circumstances was negligent. If the psychiatrist is considering prescription of the same drug under similar circumstances, the case will provide some guidance. If, as is much more frequently the case, there is no ruling on point, the legal issue (whether use of the medication under the circumstances would be acceptable medical practice, i.e., not negligent) will be re-solved by reference to medical standards. The opinions of other practitioners, articles in medical journals or treatises, drug manufacturers' recommendations, and guidelines in the Physicians Desk Reference will all be relevant. In short, to determine the legal risks of drug therapy, a psychiatrist will usually need to turn to traditional medical sources.

Another frequent claim is that the drug was administered after an inadequate examination. It would be advisable to take a complete medical history and perform a thorough physical examination (or arrange for this to be done) for any patient for whom medications are to be prescribed. However, this is sometimes not done in private practice because of a lack of necessary equipment, facilities, and assistance. Although there are few reported decisions finding psychiatrists liable on these grounds, the practice does present a risk. The risk is especially great if the patient has pre-existing health problems or if the therapeutic and potentially harmful levels of the medication are not very far apart. Thorough medical histories and examinations as well as continued monitoring of the need for medication should be conducted in these circumstances.

Negligent drug treatment cases may also be based on a failure to adequately monitor or to give adequate warnings about significant side effects. It is advisable not only to warn about a significant side effect (for example, drowsiness) but also to warn about related consequences (e.g., that it is risky to drive). In addition, all patients should be told to advise the psychiatrist whenever they experience any side effects or physical symptoms after beginning a course of drug treatment. This may stop a minor side effect from developing into a serious one and will permit a reassessment of the medication chosen if effects, including those about which the psychiatrist has not specifically advised, occur.

Finally, relatives of patients who have committed suicide by taking overdoses of medication frequently file suit claiming that the psychiatrist acted negligently in prescribing dangerous drugs (21). There is always a risk of suit after the death or serious injury of a patient, and the prescribing psychiatrist should assess carefully the risk of suicide and consider carefully the size of the prescription. However, as will be discussed at greater length below, liability does not automatically result when a patient uses drugs prescribed by the psychiatrist to commit suicide. A patient determined to commit suicide can circumvent almost any precaution used in prescribing medications. Imposing liability regardless of the circumstances or precautions would undoubtedly seriously inhibit the prescription of potentially beneficial drugs. In recognition of their benefits and of the limited control in an outpatient situation (22), courts have scrutinized circumstances carefully to determine if the prescription was negligent. To date, psychiatrists have generally prevailed in drug overdose cases involving outpatients. One commentator has suggested that the psychiatrist should be held liable only "when, in situations where the risks of suicide are great, he writes a prescription ordering a number of pills which could be fatal if taken in one dose and the patient uses the pills to commit suicide" (23). Although this test has not been specifically adopted by any court, the risk of liability would appear to be greatest under these circumstances.

Psychiatrists frequently ask about phoning in refill orders for patients of colleagues for whom they are covering. This obviously entails a greater risk for a psychiatrist than prescribing for one's own patients, when the general risk of suicide and the patient's mental state at the time are known. The best practice would be to obtain from the treating psychiatrist a list of patients who may need refills and discuss each. If, for some reason, this cannot be done, no more than a minimal amount of a potentially harmful medication should be prescribed until the treating psychiatrist can be consulted.

Tardive dyskinesia. Concern about tardive dyskinesia seems to be uppermost in the minds of many psychiatrists who regularly prescribe antipsychotic medications. Although there have as yet been few reported decisions involving tardive dyskinesia, in light of the seriousness and frequency of this side effect and the size of the damage awards that have been reported (24), this concern does not appear to be misplaced. The medical reports suggest that tardive dyskinesia occurs very infrequently and often remits spontaneously if the medications are taken for only short periods of time (25), but the risk is much more substantial with extended treatment. The best estimates suggest that about 10 to 20 percent of patients treated with anti-psychotics for more than a year suffer from tardive dyskinesia (26). In at least a substantial number of these cases, the disease is irreversible.

Allegations of negligence in cases involving tardive dyskinesia will be similar to those in other drug treatment cases. The potential for liability will be created by prescribing without an adequate history, physical examination, or laboratory evaluation; prescription of an inappropriate drug or wrong dosage or for an inappropriate interval; failure to monitor or treat side effects; failure to anticipate and control drug reactions or interactions; and failure to consult with experts as appropriate. Because of the seriousness of tardive dyskinesia, the practitioner who prescribes antipsychotics associated with the disorder should be careful to follow these steps where they are appropriate.

Likewise, in view of the seriousness of tardive dyskinesia, there is an especially great potential for liability on informed consent grounds. Faced with a patient who has developed tardive dyskinesia, it is unlikely that any court would find that it was not a risk that needed to be disclosed and explained in order to secure an effective consent. A prescribing psychiatrist should therefore be careful to disclose the risk of tardive dyskinesia, describe the symptoms, discuss the degree of risk (i.e., the incidence), explain that the condition may be irreversible, and give the patient adequate opportunity to ask questions.

Although aware of the risk involved in proceeding without effective consent, many psychiatrists have described circumstances in which they are unwilling to defer treatment until they have obtained such consent. First, many want to begin therapy without disclosing the risk of tardive dyskinesia when they believe that, because of impaired mental condition, the patient would not consent if told of the risk. Second, many psychiatrists wish to treat after obtaining consent despite serious questions about the patient's competence to consent. In both situations, psychiatrists claim that the patient would clearly consent if the condition were under control and that commencing treatment without delay is the way to bring this about.

Even though motivated by the best of humanitarian concerns, providing treatment that may cause serious side effects without obtaining informed consent always entails a risk. Should the psychiatrist decide to proceed despite the risk, however, steps can be taken to minimize it. Most importantly, as soon as the patient's symptoms are under control and questions about his or her competence dispelled, informed consent to continued treatment should be sought. The patient's consent at this point should largely protect the psychiatrist against liability for tardive dyskinesia that develops subsequently. In addition, the psychiatrist may gain some extra protection by explaining the treatment and securing consent from a spouse or close relative when the patient is incapable of granting consent.

A final note of caution is appropriate with respect to the administration of medication. Psychiatrists are often asked to prescribe drugs to patients who are being treated by nonphysician providers or by nonpsychiatric physicians. To do so without examining the patient is fraught with peril. A psychiatrist who prescribes medication is responsible for such treatment even though another provider may be primarily responsible for the overall care of the patient. The psychiatrist should, therefore, take the same precautions in these circumstances as when prescribing medication for patients who are solely his or her responsibility.

LIABILITY FOR ABANDONMENT: CREATION AND TERMINATION OF THE PHYSICIAN–PATIENT RELATIONSHIP

A psychiatrist in private practice generally has no duty to treat a patient unless he or she has agreed to do so (27). Once the psychiatrist has agreed (explicitly or implicitly), however, he or she is legally and ethically obligated to continue to provide treatment until the relationship is terminated in a proper manner. The psychiatrist who ignores this requirement and abruptly terminates treatment will be vulnerable to an abandonment charge if harm to the patient results from the termination.

The steps necessary to discharge a psychiatrist's legal and ethical duties in this regard depend to some extent on the circumstances. If there is no emergency or threatened crisis, the psychiatrist can safely terminate if the patient is given reasonable notice, assisted in finding another therapist, and if the psychiatrist provides records and information as requested by the new therapist and the patient (28). To substantiate these steps, it is advisable to supplement verbal notice with written notice to the patient.

Unfortunately, there is no hard and fast rule as to how much notice is required. In rural or other areas where it may be difficult to find a replacement, it would be advisable to give longer notice than in an area where there are many other therapists. If the patient does not locate another therapist for some reason (including the patient's refusal to cooperate), the psychiatrist is not required to continue treating the patient indefinitely. In response to a psychiatrist who asked whether he would be abandoning his Medicaid patients whom he had given 90 days notice of his retirement but was having great difficulty placing, an APA ethical opinion said, "No. Ninety days written announcement is quite adequate. . . . [Y]ou have done all you can be expected to do" (29). In such circumstances, patients should be made aware of emergency facilities available in the area.

A psychiatrist needs to be more careful when treating a patient in an emergency or crisis period. Psychiatrists frequently ask whether they can avoid liability by terminating treatment with a patient they feel is suicidal or may harm a third party. Termination under such circumstances is likely to have the opposite effect. A patient in crisis, who feels abandoned by the therapist, may commit an act that would not otherwise have been committed. In addition, a court is less likely to find that a doctor has adequately discharged his or her responsibility to a patient when services have been withheld at the time they are most needed. A psychiatrist should be very cautious in terminating during an emergency and should consider postponing termination if possible.

Without a physician–patient relationship, there is potential for neither malpractice liability nor for abandonment. Therefore, care should be taken that such a relationship is not inadvertently created and that its absence is clear to the party in question. For example, in order to permit the psychiatrist to decide whether he or she wishes to treat a patient after an initial visit, the psychiatrist should make it clear at the time of the initial contact that the first appointment is merely an opportunity for both the psychiatrist and the patient to see if they wish to establish a treatment relationship. If this is not done, the psychiatrist may be obligated to help the patient find a new doctor and remain available in the interim. Similarly, if a psychiatrist sees a patient only for purposes of evaluation (for example, at the request of an employer or as part of a military entrance exam), but the patient seems to consider the relationship as more, it would be advisable to clarify the situation in writing if it looks as if the would-be patient is likely to be litigious.

LIABILITY FOR PATIENTS' ACTS OF VIOLENCE

As a general rule, one person has no duty to control the conduct of a second person so as to prevent that person from causing physical harm to a third (30). Traditionally this rule was applied to psychiatrists, and they were not held responsible for their patients' violent acts. In the last 10 years this has changed; it is now likely that a person harmed by a psychiatric patient will attempt to hold the psychiatrist responsible for the patient's violent acts.

At the current time, the likelihood of liability is greatest when the potential victim was known to, or readily identifiable by, the psychiatrist. *Tarasoff v. Regents of the University of California* (31), the first case holding an outpatient therapist responsible for a patient's violence, involved such a victim. Prosenjit Poddar, the patient in *Tarasoff*, had been a student at the University of California and under treatment with a University psychologist, who became convinced that he might try to kill

Tatiana Tarasoff. The psychologist had the campus police detain Poddar in order to permit the initiation of civil commitment. The police interviewed Poddar, found him rational and released him. After reviewing the case, the supervising psychiatrist concluded that there was no basis for commitment. Poddar terminated treatment; two months later he killed Tatiana Tarasoff.

Tarasoff's parents sued the psychologist, the psychiatrist, and the University, claiming that they had a duty to do more—including warning her directly—to protect her from Poddar. The California Supreme Court agreed, stating:

> [O]nce a therapist does in fact determine, or under applicable professional standards should have determined, that a patient poses a serious danger of violence to others, he bears a duty to exercise reasonable care to protect the foreseeable victim of that danger.

Although the court did not limit the duty to readily identifiable victims, it focused on the duty to warn, noting that warnings do not involve the "dire consequences" entailed in restraints, such as commitment, that might be necessary to prevent violence against nonidentifiable victims. The uncertainty as to whether a psychiatrist has a duty when the victim is not identifiable was resolved in California in *Thompson v. County of Alameda* (32). The California Supreme Court held that a "precondition to liability" is an intended victim who is "readily identifiable" (33).

The judicial response to cases filed in the wake of *Tarasoff* has been varied. A number of courts have followed *Tarasoff*, holding a therapist responsible for not warning an identifiable victim, but not deciding whether the duty would be limited in this fashion or whether it would be extended to a duty to protect the general public from potential violence done by a patient. This approach was followed by the New Jersey Superior Court in *McIntosh v. Milano*, (34) which held that the family of a woman killed by a psychiatric outpatient could sue and recover from the treating psychiatrist. Courts in Kansas and Michigan have also ruled specifically that psychiatrists have a duty to warn readily identifiable victims (35). A number of other courts, faced with the issue of whether psychiatrists have a duty to protect society in general from violent patients, found that no such duty existed, but acknowledged that psychiatrists may have a duty to warn identifiable victims (36).

Brady v. Hopper, supra, is illustrative of the facts and issues before this latter group of courts and the legal approaches they have taken. In this case against John Hinckley's former psychiatrist, plaintiffs—who had been injured when Hinckley attempted to assassinate President Reagan—contended that had Dr. Hopper not been negligent in examining, diagnosing, and treating Hinckley, he would have controlled his patient's behavior and there would have been no assassination attempt. According to plaintiffs, Dr. Hopper knew or should have known that Hinckley was a danger to himself or others, because Hopper had or had access to information indicating that Hinckley identified with the assassin in the film Taxi Driver, was collecting information on political assassination, and possessed firearms. Therefore, Dr. Hopper should have hospitalized Hinckley, warned law enforcement officials of the potential for assassination, and warned his parents of his condition.

The court acknowledged that under certain circumstances therapists have a duty to protect third parties from harm but said that the duty was measured by the foreseeability of the risk. The court concluded that injuries to Brady and the other plaintiffs were not foreseeable and, therefore, there was no duty to the plaintiffs. The court emphasized that there was no allegation that Hinckley had, in talking to his psychiatrist, threatened President Reagan or anyone else. It concluded that the " 'specific threats to specific victims' rule states a workable, reasonable and fair boundary upon the sphere of a therapist's liabiity to third persons for the acts of their patients."

Courts have occasionally imposed other limitations on recovery. For example, recovery has been denied for property damage and to a patient suing her psychiatrist for not preventing her from committing a violent act (37). A number of courts have refused to require a psychiatrist to warn a victim who was already aware of the danger. The patient in Heltsley v. Votteler, supra, for example, had threatened the plaintiff and tried to run her down. The plaintiff admitted this and her knowledge of the patient's prior aggressive behavior but contended that only a warning by a professional, such as a psychiatrist, would have made her appreciate the gravity of the situation. The Iowa Supreme Court rejected the argument and refused to impose liability (38).

Other courts have disagreed. The victim in *Jablonski v. United States, supra,* had received warnings about the patient from a psychological hotline, her attorney, her priest, and her mother and had voiced her fears of the patient to defendant psychiatrists. The court held that this was not an adequate defense in a suit against the psychiatrists for failure to warn (39).

Still other courts that have considered *Tarasoff*-type situations have refused to follow the case. For example, *Hopewell v. Adebimpe* (40) was brought against a psychiatrist who had been concerned about *Tarasoff* and therefore warned his patient's employer that the patient felt harassed by her work situation and had threatened "to hurt somebody very seriously if the harassment does not stop." The patient sued for breach of confidentiality and the doctor defended on the basis of *Tarasoff*. The court held that the psychiatrist had an absolute obligation not to disclose confidential communications without the patient's written consent. See also *Shaw v. Glickman* (41).

Although a few courts have rejected the *Tarasoff* duty completely, more have gone beyond *Tarasoff* to hold psychiatrists liable for violent acts committed by their patients against persons not identifiable in advance. For example, in *Lipari v. Sears, Roebuck and Co.* (42), the plaintiff had been injured and her husband killed when a patient (who 30 days earlier had discontinued day treatment at a VA hospital against medical advice) fired a gun into a night club. The victims alleged that the doctors should have tried to commit the patient. The court refused to dismiss the suit. Noting the broad language in *Tarasoff*, the court refused to rule that "a reasonable therapist would never be required to take precautions other than warnings, or that there is never a duty to attempt to detain a patient." Other courts have ruled similarly (43).

These cases clearly impose a broader and potentially more troubling obligation on the psychiatrist. When there is a duty to an identifiable victim, it may be discharged through a warning. But when a duty to prevent random violence toward unidentified members of the public is imposed, a warning will no longer suffice. There is no victim to warn and most police departments feel their hands are tied if no crime has been committed. Instead, the psychiatrist will have to restrain the patient directly in some manner. This means the psychiatrist will have to reconsider treatment decisions regarding commitment, passes, discharges, and the use of restraints, etc., and may have to adopt a treatment that otherwise would have been rejected.

In addition to extending liability to acts of violence committed against persons not identifiable in advance, one court has extended liability to the employer of a psychiatrist whose patient *unintentionally* harmed another. The patient in *Peterson v. Washington* (44) had been discharged from a state hospital after emergency detention and short-term commitment occasioned by a schizophrenic reaction to drugs. Five days after discharge, while under the influence of drugs, the patient ran a red light at an estimated speed of 50 to 60 miles per hour and struck the plaintiff's automobile, injuring the plaintiff. The Supreme Court of Washington concluded that the psychiatrist incurred a duty to take reasonable precautions to protect anyone who might foreseeably be endangered by the patient's drug-related problems. It did not distinguish between intentional and unintentional foreseeable harm, thus establishing probably the broadest potential for psychiatric liability to date.

Whatever the extent of the duty imposed by a court, a psychiatrist will not be held liable for a patient's violent acts unless a court or jury finds both that 1) the psychiatrist determined (or under professional standards reasonably should have determined) that the patient posed a danger to another (whether identifiable or unidentifiable) and that 2) the psychiatrist did not take adequate steps to prevent the violence. When these factors have not been established, the psychiatrist has not been held liable despite the court's adoption of *Tarasoff* or extension of liability beyond *Tarasoff*. Thus, in *McIntosh v. Milano, supra*, an early post-*Tarasoff* case, the New Jersey Superior Court held that the family of a woman killed by an outpatient could sue the patient's psychiatrist but remanded the case for a determination of whether the psychiatrist should have known that the patient presented a danger to the woman in question. The evidence showed that although the patient had shown strong jealous feelings about the woman and revealed that he had fired a BB gun at her automobile, he had never disclosed any violent feelings toward her or intention to harm her. The jury decided in favor of the psychiatrist. The psychiatrist was exonerated for similar reasons in *Johnson v. United States, supra.*

However, other cases are troubling because of the court's apparent willingness to reach to find that the psychiatrist knew or should have known that the patient posed a danger to another. For example, in *Davis v. Yong-Oh Lhim, supra* the evidence that the patient posed a threat to his mother consisted of a hospital record that made reference to "threatening his mother for money," which had been made at another hospital two years earlier. See also *Jablonski v. United States, supra* (45).

These cases and the legal analyses applied point to a number of steps psychiatrists can take to minimize the risk that they will be held liable for a patient's violent acts. Some of these steps are intended to prevent violent acts from occurring, others to provide additional information and input that will assist the psychiatrist in deciding what to do and refute allegations that the psychiatrist was negligent (i.e., that he or she should have determined that the patient was dangerous, or should have taken some step that he or she failed to take).

First, obtain prior treatment records. This will generally give the treating psychiatrist more information to work with and may help place a threat or a single act of violence in context.

Second, the decision-making process should be well documented. A complete record can help establish that all relevant sources of information were consulted and all relevant factors considered in deciding whether the patient posed a risk and if so, what steps were appropriate. A record that includes this information and explains why a decision was made will help establish that the decision was reasonable even if it turns out to have been wrong.

Third, when in doubt about whether to issue a warning or take other steps to avert harm, a psychiatrist should arrange (and document) a consultation with a second clinician and/or an attorney. A psychiatrist's liability in this context will be determined by reference to the standards of the profession.

Consulting another psychiatrist—setting out the facts and seeking advice as to the degree of danger—should, therefore, provide some extra protection. Consulting an attorney as to legal standards and obligations thereunder should also assist in decision making and help establish that due care was taken.

Fourth, when a psychiatrist determines that there is a danger of violence to an identifiable person, all appropriate warnings should be made, even if the psychiatrist is certain that the victim is aware of the danger. Each case should be considered separately to determine if others, such as parents or spouses, should be contacted in addition to (or instead of) the identified victim.

Fifth, when in doubt about whether a patient poses a danger to the public, it is advisable to initiate commitment proceedings when reasonably possible. Responsibility then passes to the judge, who will not be held liable if he or she decides not to commit a patient who later harms someone. Where judicial process is available, it is important to remember that the decision to commit is a judicial matter, not a psychiatric matter. The responsibility of psychiatrists in this circumstance is to present the facts and medical conclusions as they know them.

Finally, upon discharging a patient who has shown the potential for violence, a psychiatrist should make certain that any treatment plan developed is actually followed and, if it is not, decide whether the patient should again be restrained. Too often psychiatrists detemine that a patient may be safely discharged if outpatient therapy continues, or if the patient stays on medication, but neglect to check that these steps are taken. At least some effort should be made to follow up on a discharged patient—by asking the outpatient psychiatrist or community mental health center to contact you if the patient stops coming.

LIABILITY FOR PATIENT SUICIDES

When a psychiatric patient commits or attempts suicide the treating psychiatrist is often sued by family members or, in the case of an unsuccessful attempt, the injured patient. In the study of claims filed between 1972 and 1983 against psychiatrists covered by the APA-sponsored professional liability insurance, such cases accounted for 20% of all claims (46).

These cases usually fall into one of three categories. First, when a hospitalized patient commits suicide, the treating psychiatrist may be sued by surviving family members who claim that the psychiatrist did not provide adequate care and arrange for adequate supervision (47). Second, when a patient recently released from a hospital commits or attempts suicide, family members (or the injured patient) frequently sue the treating psychiatrist claiming that the discharge decision was negligent. Finally, a psychiatrist may be sued when an outpatient commits suicide or is injured in an attempt. Plaintiffs in these cases claim that the suicide was a result of the psychiatrist's inadequate treatment, including failure to hospitalize.

Although the fact patterns in these cases differ, courts apply the same analysis in determining liability. A treating psychiatrist will not be held liable for a patient's suicide or attempt unless a court determines 1) that the psychiatrist should have predicted that the patient was likely to harm himself or herself, and 2) that in light of the degree of risk, the psychiatrist did not take adequate steps to protect the patient. Although there is a substantial risk of liability in a suicide case, in addressing these issues many courts have shown sympathy to the psychiatrist and an appreciation of countervailing treatment considerations. They have recognized the difficulty of predicting suicide and the complexity of the treatment decision.

Suicide by Hospitalized Patients

Prediction of suicide by hospitalized patients is no easier than in other contexts. Most psychiatrists do not claim to be able to predict accurately the probability that a particular patient will attempt suicide. Even prior attempts are not an invariably reliable guide (48). Thus, predictive errors will be made despite the psychiatrist's exercise of due and reasonable care.

This has led a number of courts to rule in favor of psychiatrists whose judgments have proven to be incorrect. According to these courts, a psychiatrist should not be held liable if a decision was reasonable and based on sufficient information (49). Other courts have been less reluctant to impose liability, especially in light of a prior suicide attempt (50) or a failure to diagnose a condition that increased the probability of suicide (51).

When the risk of suicide has been recognized by the psychiatrist but the act or attempt not prevented, courts assess the adequacy of precautionary measures ordered by the psychiatrist. This is a complex issue for both the psychiatrist and the court. Increasing observation, placing the patient in seclusion, or using physical and chemical restraints will probably reduce the short term risk of suicide (52). But such measures may also prolong the patient's illness, delay discharge, and increase the risk of suicide at some later time.

In a number of recent cases, courts have recognized that permitting a patient a certain amount of freedom may be therapeutic and increasing precautions may be anti-therapeutic. Concluding that the risks and benefits of increased freedom should be balanced by the psychiatrist, they have been willing to defer to his or her judgment, even though it later appears to have been wrong (53). In a few cases, however, courts have refused to defer to the psychiatrist's conclusions about the adequacy of precautions. Findings of liability are frequently based on the conclusion that the psychiatrist underestimated the risk and, thereby, the need for special precautions.

As in other malpractice cases, the reasonableness of the psychiatrist's conclusions about these issues will be tested against the standards of the profession. Thus, the risk of liability will be greatest when the plaintiff produces experts who testify that the psychiatrist did not exercise reasonable care. There is also a substantial risk of liability when the psychiatrist fails to follow his or her own usual practices in caring for a patient at risk for suicide and cannot explain the deviation (54).

Suicide Following Discharge from a Hospital

Courts considering a suicide or an attempt following an inpatient's release must make essentially the same determinations: Whether a psychiatrist exercising reasonable skill would have 1) foreseen the risk of suicide and 2) if so, concluded that the benefits to be derived from discharge outweighed the risks. The latter is a particularly complex decision for a psychiatrist. While extending hospitalization may reduce the risk of suicide, it also reduces the likelihood that the patient will be able to resume a normal life outside the institution—the psychiatrist's ultimate goal. Most psychiatrists believe that there are clear therapeutic benefits to a prompt release. In a particular case, a psychiatrist's decision will undoubtedly depend on an assessment of factors such as the level of the risk of suicide, the ability of the patient to care for himself or herself or to receive assistance from others, the extent to which the illness is in remission and can be controlled by medication or other outpatient treatment, and the support the patient will receive in the circumstances into which he or she is being released. In making such assessments and balancing such unmeasurable factors, errors of judgment are inevitable.

The difficulties of prediction and the generally accepted benefits of release have been recognized by a number of courts in recent years. In ruling against plaintiffs, the court in *Johnson v. United States* (55), said,

> [M]odern psychiatry has recognized the importance of making every effort to return a patient to an active and productive life. Thus the patient is encouraged to develop his self-confidence by adjusting to the demands of everyday existence. Particularly because the prediction of danger is difficult, undue reliance on hospitalization might lead to prolonged incarceration of potentially useful members of society.

The court in *Fiederlein v. City of New York Health and Hospitals Corporation* (56) showed similar deference to the psychiatrist's judgment in release decisions. The court pointed out that if psychiatrists were found liable for every incorrect prediction, they would be very unwilling to release patients and the rehabilitation of many patients would be frustrated (57).

Not all courts have been willing to defer to the psychiatrist's judgment, however. As in other malpractice cases, the likelihood of a court imposing liability is particularly great when it determines a psychiatrist failed to conduct a proper medical examination, neglected to consult readily available sources of information about the patient, or failed to consider an important factor that was known or available to him or her (58).

Suicide by Outpatients

The decisions a court must make in an outpatient suicide case are similar to those discussed above: (l) Whether a psychiatrist should have recognized that a patient presented a risk of suicide, and (2) whether the psychiatrist was negligent in balancing the risk of suicide against the benefits of increasd control. However, the situation is different for the psychiatrist because it is much more difficult to control the potentially suicidal outpatient. The psychiatrist's options—and the degree of control they give—are quite limited. With a patient undergoing psychotherapy, the frequency of sessions may be increased or therapy may be focused on eliminating the suicidal urges. The threat of suicide may also be reduced by prescribing medication. This, however, carries its own risk of suicide. The psychiatrist may also recommend hospitalization. However, the psychiatrist cannot force the patient to enter the hospital unless the risk of suicide is clear enough to support involuntary commitment.

The strong reluctance that courts have shown to impose liability for outpatient suicides may reflect their recognition of this lack of control over the patient. *Speer v. United States* (59) is typical of outpatient suicide cases. Although an outpatient overdosed on antipsychotic drugs prescribed by the defendant, the court refused to find the psychiatrist negligent. It first found that a psychiatrist's duty to outpatients is less extensive than the duty to inpatients. It then noted that use of antipsychotic drugs was essential in the treatment of schizophrenics and that the amount prescribed by the defendant was within the limits of safe drug use (although greater than the dosage recommended by the *Physician's Desk Reference*). The court also emphasized that there had been no basis for predicting that the patient was likely to use the medication to commit suicide (60).

Reducing the Risk of Liability

A patient suicide is an event likely to trigger suit. However, a psychiatrist can take a number of steps that should reduce the risk of liability.

First, when there is a significant issue as to the degree of the risk of suicide or the appropriate treatment decision in light of that risk, a psychiatrist should consider consultation with another practitioner. This should help the psychiatrist resolve the issues in his or her own mind and also help establish that due care was taken in arriving at a treatment decision. While courts have shown themselves willing to overlook errors of judgment, they obviously have been less sympathetic when it becomes apparent that the psychiatrist did not follow procedures generally used in the profession.

Second, psychiatrists treating patients who may present some risk of suicide should be extremely careful to explain in their patient records their determinations as to the degree of risk and as to what steps are appropriate in light of that risk. The records should indicate what sources of information were consulted, what factors considered in arriving at a decision, and how the factors were balanced (61). Such a record should go a long way toward convincing a court or jury that a decision, although ultimately wrong, was not arrived at carelessly or thoughtlessly.

Third, when treating an outpatient who refuses hospitalization or an inpatient who insists on leaving, psychiatrists who determine that the risk of suicide seems sufficiently great that hospitalization appears to be the only reliable method of prevention should consider initiating involuntary commitment. As in the dangerous patient situation, if the court finds that the patient does not present a sufficient risk, the psychiatrist would be protected in the event of a future suicide.

Fourth, if a patient appears to present a risk of suicide, a psychiatrist should try to obtain information about possible prior attempts from all available sources. Although the predictive value of prior attempts is far from clear, it is a factor that courts have relied on to the detriment of the defendant.

Finally, much as in the dangerous patient case, a psychiatrist who discharges a potentially suicidal patient should do sufficient follow-up to determine that the patient is receiving outpatient treatment and/or medication.

CONSENT TO TREATMENT

Informed Consent

Like other doctors, a psychiatrist must obtain a patient's consent before providing medical treatment. In order for the patient's consent to be effective (i.e., to protect the doctor against charges of battery or negligence), it must be in-formed—given after the patient has received a fair and reason-able explanation of the proposed treatment.

The standard for a legally sufficient disclosure varies from state to state. Traditionally, the duty of disclosure has been measured by a professional standard: either the customary disclosure practices of physicians or what a reasonable physi-cian would disclose under similar circumstances. In recent years, however, a growing number of courts have applied a *patient-oriented* disclosure standard. This standard focuses not on what the physician thinks the patient should know, but on what "material" information about risks a reasonable person in the patient's situation would want to know in order to make a reasonably informed decision.

Even in patient-centered jurisdictions, a physician needs to disclose only material risks, not all possible risks. A material risk is typically defined as one which a physician knows or should know would be significant to a reasonable person in the patient's situation (62). Factors frequently identified as relevant in determining whether a risk is material include the severity of the risk, the likelihood of injurious side effects or death, the need for treatment, and the availability of compara-ble and less dangerous alternatives. If a particular treatment is clearly necessary and the risks minimal, less than complete disclosure may be permissible. On the other hand, where a particular treatment is especially intrusive or dangerous, a court is likely to be more demanding about disclosure.

In an attempt to both protect patients and provide some certainty for practitioners, some states have begun to enact informed consent legislation. The Texas law is representative. It sets out over 50 procedures for which no warning beyond the general risks of anesthesia and surgery are required. For an additional set of 30 to 40 procedures, it specifies what risks must be spelled out and requires that they be set out in writing. At the current time the guidelines are not mandatory. However, it is expected that those who follow the guidelines will be protected against charges that they failed to disclose material risks.

Whatever standard of disclosure applies, the plaintiff in an informed consent case must establish that the failure to inform adequately of the risk was the cause of the harm. Generally the patient must prove that if a reasonable person had been given the omitted information, such a person would have not gone ahead with the procedure. More patient-oriented courts may allow patients to prove that they themselves would not have consented if they had had the information.

Under certain circumstances, disclosing risks to the patient and obtaining consent may not be necessary. A psychiatrist should be cautious about relying on most of these exceptions: support for them is sparse and courts are unlikely to dramatically expand exceptions that could swallow the doctrine of informed consent.

First, there is a generally recognized exception for emergencies. Almost any rational person facing an acute, life-threatening crisis demanding immediate treatment would consent to treatment. Accordingly, the law will infer consent in such a crisis, when the patient is incapable of either receiving information or giving consent, and there is insufficient time to obtain consent from a legally designated substitute decision-maker. Especially if psychiatrists anticipate that the administration of antipsychotics on an emergency basis may be required, they should familiarize themselves with any statutes, regulations, or judicial opinions in their jurisdictions that define *emergency* for these purposes.

Second, in certain circumstances physicians may have *therapeutic privilege* to withhold information if they determine that a complete disclosure of possible risks and alternatives might have a significantly detrimental effect on a patient's physical or psychological welfare. The privilege may apply when disclosure would increase the risk of treatment itself or would interfere with the patient's decision-making process. However, a physician may not invoke the privilege merely because of fears that the patient would refuse the treatment if informed of the risk. Jurisdictions vary as to the physician's discretion in invoking the privilege and his or her duty to disclose withheld information to a legally designated substitute decision maker.

In general, psychiatrists should be very cautious about relying on this exception without a clear, recent judicial opinion approving the privilege. Courts have become more sensitive to preserving a patient's autonomy and are moving in the direction of requiring more, rather than less, complete disclosures. If deciding to rely on the therapeutic privilege, psychiatrists should record why they concluded that full disclosure would harm this particular patient (even though it would ordinarily not harm other patients). They may also gain some extra protection by obtaining consent from a close relative of the patient.

Third, there is generally said to be an exception to the requirement of informed consent when the patient is not competent, because an incompetent is, by legal definition, incapable of giving informed consent. However, if informed consent would be required for a particular treatment, it must be obtained from a substitute decision maker, which is frequently more onerous and involves greater uncertainties for the psychiatrist. This requirement in the medical and outpatient psychiatric context is discussed below.

Finally, there is an exception for waivers. A physician need not disclose risks of treatment when the patient has specifically requested that he or she not be told. Because waivers of legal rights are typically required to be "knowing" and "voluntary," the psychiatrist who plans to rely on this exception must make certain that patients realize they have a right to the information and willingly give up this right. This may present some of the same problems as does determining whether the patient is competent. If the psychiatrist is concerned that a waiver may be a product of a patient's illness, it would be advisable to seek consent of a relative.

Consent in General Medical and Outpatient Psychiatric Contexts: Competency and Substituted Consent

Psychiatrists are often asked by other physicians in a hospital setting to evaluate the competency of patients who refuse needed treatment. In addition, because only competent patients can give informed consent, psychiatrists must satisfy themselves that patients who consent to a course of psychiatric treatment are competent. In close cases, it is advisable to cover the issue of competency in the patient's record. A consultation with another psychiatrist would provide additional protection.

Persons are considered competent to make decisions about

their medical care if they have "sufficient mind to reasonably understand the condition, the nature and effect of the proposed treatment, attendant risks in pursuing the treatment, and not pursuing the treatment" from In the Matter of William Schiller (63).

A physician who treats a patient who refuses treatment, or who consents but whose competence is in question, risks liability unless one of the exceptions discussed above is available. This will usually mean obtaining the consent of a substitute decision maker. For maximum protection, the provider should follow the state's statutorily defined procedures for the adjudication of incompetency and establishment of a guardianship (64).

Because these procedures are time consuming and may delay treatment, psychiatrists frequently ask if there is any legal basis for accepting the substituted consent of a spouse or close relative. Aside from infrequent statutes that authorize consent by relatives in limited circumstances, only a few scattered cases provide support for this procedure (65). In light of this limited support and the increasing tendency of legislatures and courts to protect the rights of patients to make their own treatment decisions, it would be inadvisable to assume that courts will affirm the right of physicians to decide that a patient is in fact incompetent and to rely on a relative's consent. Two risks are involved: that the patient may later be found to have been competent and that the relative may be found to have no authority to consent. If either occurs, the physician who provided the treatment may be held liable.

The actual risk of liability may be quite small, however. To begin with, in the majority of cases, where the relative giving consent is motivated by concern for the patient and is on good terms with the patient, a suit is unlikely. Even if a suit is filed, there is a good chance the physician will not be found liable. In the many cases where the relative who consented would have been appointed guardian, ignoring the guardianship procedure will not result in treatment that would not otherwise have taken place. Thus, the causation element of a malpractice case would be missing. In addition, many courts may be reluctant to hold liable a physician who acted in good faith and within the bounds of good medical judgment as to the incompetency of the patient and the need for treatment.

LIABILITY ARISING FROM EMPLOYER, SUPERVISORY, AND CONSULTATIVE RELATIONSHIPS

Psychiatrists have professional relationships with employees and with therapists to whom they provide supervisory or consultative services. All of these relationships may subject the psychiatrist to liability.

Employer Relationships

Under traditional tort law, an employer is responsible for the wrongful acts of an employee if these acts are committed within the scope of the employee's employment. The employer is held vicariously liable even when not at fault in any way—including in the hiring and supervision of the employee. Accordingly, psychiatrists will be held liable for the negligent acts of their nurses or other employees. Psychiatrists with employees should make certain that their malpractice insurance covers such potential liability.

Supervisory Relationships

The APA's "Guidelines for Psychiatrists in Consultative, Supervisory or Collaborative Relationships with Nonmedical Therapists" states that

> [i]n a supervisory relationship the psychiatrist retains direct responsibility for patient care and gives professional direction and active guidance to the therapist. In this relationship the nonmedical therapist may be the employee of an organized health-care setting or of the psychiatrist. The psychiatrist is clinically responsible for the initial workup, diagnosis, and prescription of a treatment plan, as well as for assuring that adequate and timely attention is paid to the patient's physical status and that such information is integrated into the overall evaluation, diagnosis, and planning. Psychiatrists remain ethically and medically responsible for the patient's care as long as the treatment continues under his or her supervision. The patient should be fully informed of the existence and nature of, and any changes in, the supervisory relationship.

In a supervisory relationship, the psychiatrist will be responsible not only for diagnosis and development of the treatment plan, but also for monitoring and supervising the therapy to ensure that the plan is being properly implemented and that appropriate adjustments are made to accommodate any changes in the patient's condition. The APA guidelines state that it is difficult to specify the necessary frequency of contacts between the supervising psychiatrist and the other therapist. But it is clear that the supervisory relationship is a serious undertaking and must not be entered into lightly for insurance or other purposes. Psychiatrists who undertake such a relationship should bear in mind that they will be responsible for the patient, just as if they were the sole provider.

Consultative Relationships

The APA guidelines state that in a consultative relationship "a psychiatrist does not assume responsibility for the patient's care. The psychiatrist evaluates the information provided by the therapist and offers a medical opinion which the therapist may or may not accept . . ."

There is very little law in the area of consultative relationships and it is difficult to set forth any hard and fast rules. Speaking generally, however, the risk of liability for a psychiatrist who acts in a truly consultative capacity is probably quite small. In such a role, the psychiatrist assumes no direct medical responsibility for the patient. Instead, the psychiatrist evaluates the information provided by the other therapist and offers an opinion or advice that the therapist may or may not accept. The fact that the psychiatrist's relationship is with the therapist, not the patient, does not preclude liability in all cases. However, a consultative relationship poses far less risk of liability than a supervisory relationship.

When acting as a consultant, a psychiatrist relies on the facts presented by the therapist. Thus a psychiatrist would risk liability only if the opinion and advice given were arrived at negligently based on the limited information available to him or her.

Moreover, even where the psychiatrist is found to have acted negligently in the consulting capacity, it is still possible that he or she would not be held liable. In light of the intervening professional judgment of the treating therapist— who is, after all, completely free to disregard the psychiatrist's opinion—the psychiatrist's advice might not be found to be the cause of harm to the patient. This, however, may be less true as the professional qualifications of the therapist decline. A nonphysician provider may be regarded as less free to ignore a psychiatrist's advice than another psychiatrist, for example.

It is important to note that a psychiatrist's liability will be limited only if he or she actually functions as a consultant. If a psychiatrist is called a consultant, but in reality functions as a supervisor, he or she will have wider responsibility.

2

Confidentiality and Privilege

The obligation of confidentiality, incumbent on all physicians (66) has been of paramount concern in psychiatry.
This is reflected in the American Psychiatric Association's
ethical annotations, which provide the following:

> Confidentiality is essential to psychiatric treatment. This is based in part
> on the special nature of psychiatric therapy as well as on the traditional
> ethical relationship between physician and patient. . . . Because of the
> sensitive and private nature of the information with which the psychiatrist
> deals, he/she must be circumspect in the information that he/she
> chooses to disclose to others about a patient. The welfare of the patient
> must be a continuing consideration (67).

Most psychiatrists report that from the beginning of their
training they have been inculcated with both the profession's
ethical position on confidentiality and the necessity of confidentiality for treatment. This sensitivity has been heightened
by the relatively recent development of a body of case law
permitting patients to sue physicians and recover monetary
damages when their confidentiality has been breached. The
result is twofold. First, most psychiatrists are extremely cautious about disclosing information and frequently seek legal
advice about confidentiality issues. Second, despite (or perhaps because of) the preoccupation of most psychiatrists with

confidentiality, suits for disclosure of confidential information are relatively rare. In the study of claims made against psychiatrists covered by the APA-sponsored professional liability insurance, only 3 percent were based on breach of confidentiality (68).

The sections below will discuss the ethical and legal duty of confidentiality and the related concept of privilege. There is frequently confusion about these concepts. *Privilege* is a rule of evidence and applies only in a judicial context. When a communication is privileged, the holder of the privilege (here, the patient) may prevent the person to whom the information was given (the physician) from disclosing it in a judicial proceeding. In the context of the physician-patient relationship, confidentiality refers to the duty of the physician not to disclose information learned directly or indirectly from the patient to anyone not directly involved in the patient's case.

PHYSICIAN–PATIENT AND PSYCHOTHERAPIST PATIENT PRIVILEGE

Coverage of Statutes

Currently every state except South Carolina has enacted some form of physician–patient or psychotherapist–patient privilege. However, there is great variation among the statutes as to which providers are covered and the circumstances in which the privilege may be exercised.

Psychiatrists frequently ask whether the nonphysician providers whom they supervise or their assistants are included within the physician–patient privilege. It is very unlikely that a psychologist, social worker, etc. would be found to be covered by a physician–patient privilege statute merely because supervised by a psychiatrist. For those staff members considered assistants, there is no general rule. However, in the absence of a specific statutory provision (69), most courts have extended the privilege to those considered to be the physician's agent (i.e., to people who act under the direction and supervision of the physician) (70).

The privilege generally extends not only to qualifying patient communications, but also to information learned in the course of examination or treatment (71) and to the physician's conclusions and diagnosis (72). However, not all communications or information are covered. To begin with, courts have required a clear connection between the communication and the provision of treatment. In a psychiatric context, where patients must speak of whatever is on their minds if treatment is to succeed, this should present no problem. It is likely that any communication made to a psychiatrist within a treatment relationship would be within the privilege. However, disclosures made for purposes other than obtaining treatment, including disclosures made in the course of a personal relationship, are not covered by the privilege. Thus, examination undertaken for reasons other than treatment—such as qualifying for employment or insurance or pursuant to court order—will usually not be privileged. In a number of states the privilege will also be lost if third parties are present when the disclosure is made (73). However, it will generally be maintained if the third parties are close family members of the patient or employees of the physician present to facilitate treatment (74).

There is considerable disagreement among courts as to the coverage of information received from members of the patient's family and other third parties. Information from family members may be very important to psychiatric treatment and there may be reluctance to provide it if confidentiality is not assured. Some courts have demonstrated sensitivity to these concerns (75).

Waiver of the Privilege

If the patient or a person authorized to act for the patient waives the privilege, information that would otherwise be excluded may be introduced in court. Statutes and judicial opinions should be consulted to determine who has the right of waiver. Generally speaking, if an adult is alive and legally competent, only he or she may execute a valid waiver. If the patient has been declared legally incompetent, a guardian must be consulted. In some states, a guardian *ad litem*—whose power extends only to the judicial proceedings—may be appointed by the court to decide the question when the patient is mentally incapacitated but has not yet been declared legally incompetent.

If the patient is a minor, waiver decisions are generally made by the parent or legal guardian. One parent's waiver is generally sufficient, but care should be taken in a custody dispute where the parents may disagree about whether to waive the privilege. There has been some recent judicial recognition of the interests affecting waiver in the custody context. For example, in Nagle v. Hooks (76), the court held that when the minor is too young to make decisions about the exercise or waiver of the privilege, the court must appoint a guardian to act in the child's interests and the parents, either alone or together, may not agree or refuse to waive the privilege on the child's behalf.

An adolescent patient may hold the right of waiver in certain situations. Most states have given adolescents the right to control the release of medical information in at least limited circumstances. The adolescent should have a corresponding right to control the privilege in those circumstances (77).

Any state law requirements regarding the form and content of a waiver should be observed (78). Even when an oral waiver would suffice under state law, it would be advisable to obtain a written one whenever circumstances permit. The process of executing a waiver will force the patient to focus on the issue. In addition, there will be documentation of the patient's decision.

Courts have also recognized implied waivers. For example, a patient who testifies about privileged communications may not prevent a physician from doing so (79). A valid waiver in another case or disclosure of privileged matters outside of court may be held to be a permanent waiver. In addition, some courts have held that when a patient calls a physician to testify about an illness or injury, the patient thereby waives privilege with respect to any other physician consulted about the same condition. At the current time there is no clear rule as to whether a patient waives by testifying about his or her condition at the time the communications in question were made.

Exceptions to the Privilege

Both statutory and judicially developed exceptions to the privilege are common. Those most frequently relevant in a psychiatric context are exceptions that apply when the patient's medical condition is the issue, in a civil commitment proceeding, in a will contest, in a child custody dispute, and when the physician has filed a report required by law.

Frequently privilege statutes specifically state that the privilege is not available when the patient has put his or her condition in issue in a lawsuit. Even in the absence of such a provision, courts often find that by putting his or her condition in issue, the patient has waived the privilege (80). However, courts often disagree about when a patient has in fact, placed his or her condition in issue. Asking for damages for pain and suffering is enough to put the litigant's mental condition in issue in some states but not in others (81). There is also disagreement as to whether a parent waives privilege by contesting child custody (82).

Many state privilege statutes contain exceptions for civil commitment proceedings. The same result is reached in other states by court findings that the condition-in-issue exception applies or that the privilege does not apply in commitment proceedings.

There is a large body of law addressing who may waive the privilege in litigation between a patient's estate and a third party. Most frequently the legal representative, the administrator, or the patient's heir is held to have this power. The situation is more complicated in a will contest where both sides claim to represent the deceased but one side is likely to want to waive the privilege while the other will wish to assert it. Where this has been addressed by statute, full disclosure has been favored: Some statutes permit either party to waive the privilege (83), others simply create an exception to the general privilege in these circumstances (84).

Some states specifically limit the privilege in child custody cases. In Massachusetts, for example, there is an exception when the judge, after a hearing in chambers, decides that the psychotherapist has evidence that bears significantly on the parents' ability to provide custody and it is more important to the child's welfare that the communication be disclosed than that the physician–patient relationship be protected (85). This exception for child custody cases is somewhat atypical, resting on the paramount interests of the child. Even in this area, however, some courts are willing to uphold the privilege and rely instead on an independent psychiatric examination.

Almost every state code requires physicians to report certain occurrences or conditions (e.g., child abuse, diseases associated with the loss of consciousness, gunshot wounds, communicable diseases) even though they have been learned through a confidential relationship. A few state statutes specifically provide for such an exception; in other states, the exception is usually implicit in the statutory provisions.

Finally, in recent years, several courts have ruled that the doctor–patient privilege does not protect a physician who is subpoenaed in a criminal investigation involving the physician. Usually, disclosure in such cases is limited to the names and treatment dates of patients, although it is possible that these areas will be broadened in future cases.

Determining Whether Privilege Applies

As this discussion illustrates, whether or not the privilege will be found to apply and to prohibit the physician from providing testimony in a given case is far from clear. Privilege provisions vary substantially from state to state, and individual courts are continually engrafting on their own exceptions and implied waivers and balancing interests according to their individual values. Once a psychiatrist provides information in the belief that the privilege does not apply, it is difficult to reclaim the privilege and protect the interests behind it if this belief turns out to be wrong. Thus, it is important that a psychiatrist proceed as if the privilege prevented him from providing information unless it is clear that it does not apply. In most cases, therefore, it is advisable to follow the general rules for responding to a subpoena. These rules are discussed in the next section.

RESPONDING TO A SUBPOENA

Psychiatrists frequently ask how to respond when they are subpoenaed to appear at a trial or deposition or to make their records available. As a general matter, any person subpoenaed is required to provide relevant testimony about matters within his or her knowledge. However, there are countervailing ethical and legal considerations when a physician is subpoenaed to testify about a patient. As discussed above, in most states there is a physician–patient or psychotherapist–patient privilege that enables a patient, under certain circumstances, to prevent a psychiatrist who treated him or her from testifying about his or her condition, treatment, or confidential information disclosed in the course of that treatment. In addition, there are ethical constraints. A psychiatrist may ethically "release confidential information only with the authorization of the patient or under proper legal compulsion" (86). Violation of this principle may subject the psychiatrist both to ethical charges and to suit for breach of confidentiality.

Although it issues from a court, a subpoena is not in itself "proper legal compulsion." It compels the psychiatrist to appear, not to testify. Subpoenas are not issued by a judge; they are issued routinely by the clerk of the court on request of a lawyer. Thus, when a psychiatrist receives a subpoena, there has been as yet no consideration of claims of privilege or confidentiality that could alter the general obligation to provide evidence. A psychiatrist should take whatever steps are necessary to protect the interests of his or her patient and to make certain that no information is disclosed until the legal issues are properly resolved.

Often a subpoena will be accompanied by a consent form signed by the patient. If the consent conforms to requirements of state law and the psychiatrist is satisfied that it was informed, he or she is free to testify and to provide any documents requested. Even when the patient has consented, however, the psychiatrist is ethically obligated to disclose only information that is actually relevant. If asked about sensitive information that seems clearly irrelevant, the need for disclosure should be questioned. At a deposition, the irrelevance and sensitivity of the information sought may in some cases make it necessary for the psychiatrist to refuse to disclose the information without more specific consent from the patient or an order from the court.

If there is no consent with the subpoena, a psychiatrist may wish first to contact the patient or the patient's attorney to determine if the patient will consent to the release of information. If the patient does not consent, either the patient's attorney or the psychiatrist may file a motion to quash the subpoena on the grounds that the testimony would violate the physician–patient privilege and the physician's duty of confidentiality to the patient. The court's ruling on this motion would settle the issue of whether the psychiatrist must testify or turn over his or her records. In many cases, the psychiatrist may be able to accomplish the same result by simply writing a letter to the court, explaining the situation and asking for direction.

If no motion to quash is made, the psychiatrist is obligated to appear at the trial or place of deposition as the subpoena directs. When a psychiatrist is first asked about a patient at trial, either the patient's attorney or the psychiatrist should raise the physician–patient privilege and request the court to rule that the psychiatrist need not testify. If, having considered the confidentiality concerns, the court orders the psychiatrist to answer, the psychiatrist must either comply or risk being held in contempt.

At a deposition, much the same procedure can be followed. As soon as the first question about the patient is asked, either the psychiatrist or the patient's attorney, who will almost always be present, should say that privileged or confidential material is involved and that the psychiatrist will not answer until ordered to do so by the court. The attorneys will then arrange for the court to resolve the issue. In order to save time and avoid a pointless deposition session, the psychiatrist or the patient's attorney may wish to inform the attorney issuing the subpoena in advance that they will raise the privilege. The parties can then try to get the issue resolved before the date of the deposition.

PSYCHIATRISTS' DUTY OF CONFIDENTIALITY

Although psychiatrists have traditionally been vulnerable to ethical charges for breaching patient confidentiality, vulnerability to suit for monetary damages for such a breach is a relatively recent development. For the most part, it is a result of judicial, rather than legislative, developments. Courts have developed different legal theories to support recovery.

In several cases, courts have based recovery on a physician-patient contract, which has been found to include an implied term that the physician would keep confidential any information received from the patient (87). When this covenant has been found, recovery for the plaintiff has usually resulted. However, a plaintiff's recovery in a breach of contract suit is limited to economic losses flowing directly from the breach and will not include compensation for items such as mental distress, loss of employment, and deterioration of a marital relationship. Courts have therefore sought other bases of recovery.

Invasion of privacy has been held to support recovery in a number of cases (88). It has been defined as an ''unwarranted publicization of one's private affairs with which the public has no legitimate concern, such as to cause outrage, mental suffering, shame or humiliation to a person of ordinary sensibilities'' (89). This theory may be of limited use to a plaintiff, however, because it has traditionally been held to require a public disclosure of private facts as opposed to disclosure to an individual or a small group.

Because of these limitations, a number of courts have developed another theory of recovery (90). These courts have found that the relationship between physician and patient imposed on the physician a fiduciary duty of confidentiality that is breached by an unauthorized disclosure of confidential information. Courts have differed as to the source of the duty.

In a number of cases, patients have argued that physician licensing statutes and physician–patient privilege statutes embody a remedy for unauthorized disclosure of information. Although this argument has been accepted occasionally (91), most courts have been reluctant to permit a civil suit on the basis of these statutes (92). However, such provisions are likely to be viewed as reflecting public policy and, thus, supporting adoption of a cause of action based on tort or contract for unauthorized disclosure of confidential information.

Courts have permitted recovery for a variety of unauthorized disclosures. These have included the release of information to the patient's employer (93), unauthorized disclosures to a patient's spouse (94), the disclosure of information to an insurer or potential defendant in a personal injury action (95), and disclosure of details of psychiatric treatment in a book (96).

The defenses raised by physicians in these cases have met with varied success. A valid consent will clearly protect the physician both legally and ethically (97). However, to be valid, the consent must be knowing and voluntary. The voluntariness of consent is likely to be scrutinized closely in the psychiatric context because of the influence the psychiatrist is in a position to exert over the patient. The handling of the issue in *Doe v. Roe, supra,* is illustrative. Defendant psychiatrist, sued for writing a book about the patient's treatment in which her fantasies, memories, and feelings were recounted, claimed he had obtained the patient's consent. The court said of the defense: "This defense is without substance. Consent was sought while the plaintiff was in therapy. It was never obtained in writing. . . . I need not deal with the value of an oral waiver of confidentiality given by a patient to a psychiatrist during the course of treatment." Where disclosures are made for reasons other than the patient's benefit, as in *Doe v. Roe,* consent will be scrutinized particularly closely. A psychiatrist who wishes to rely on consent in such circumstances should obtain it in writing and may want to consider having another professional (psychiatrist or attorney) discuss the issue with the patient to establish that consent is knowing and voluntary.

Courts have been reasonably receptive in disclosure cases to the defense of an over-riding public interest. Psychiatrists who have warned third parties of potential patient violence have usually not been held liable for breach of confidentiality. Disclosures have also been found justified when necessary to protect the general public or a third party from other dangers (98). The *public interest* defense has not been accepted without careful scrutiny, however. In *Doe v. Roe, supra,* the court rejected defendant's claim that the disclosures were justified by the book's contribution to the education of the medical profession. Psychiatrists considering a public interest disclosure should weigh carefully the interests to be served by the disclosure and the patient's interest in confidentiality; there is always a risk that a court will not agree that the public interest justified the breach.

Occasionally disclosures may be justified on the grounds

the issue has been addressed by case law. If the waiver provisions are not clear, the psychiatrist should turn to the court to get the issue resolved.

Whether to assist an investigation, help a relative work through grief, or deter suit, psychiatrists often decide to disclose information after a patient's death although there is no legal support for such disclosures. When this is done the risks can usually be minimized. First, the psychiatrist should disclose the minimum necessary to accommodate the competing interest. General information about the patient's state of mind, rather than specific information about patient disclosures, may suffice for grieving family members or in a police investigation. Second, psychiatrists should be careful to not disclose any information about third parties. Third, psychiatrists may obtain some legal protection by obtaining authorization from the patient's legal representative and close family members. It is unlikely that such authorizations would make the disclosures "legal," but if the consent is informed, those giving the authorization would probably be found to have lost their right to sue.

CONFIDENTIALITY AND MINOR PATIENTS

Issues involving the confidentiality rights of minors are among the most troubling in the confidentiality area. It is clear that in many circumstances parents of minor patients are entitled to information about their children and are legally responsible for making other confidentiality decisions. However, it is also clear that minors possess an independent right of confidentiality which must be taken account of and in certain circumstances will prevail. The APA's ethical guidelines reflect the countervailing interests. They provide the following:

> Careful judgment must be exercised by the psychiatrist in order to include, when appropriate, the parents or guardian in the treatment of a minor. At the same time the psychiatrist must assure the minor proper confidentiality (101).

The issue of whether, and to what extent, minors have confidentiality rights arises in a number of contexts—whether psychiatrists are required, or permitted, to release information to a minor's parent without consent; whether it is the minor's parents who may exercise a statutory right of access to medical records; whether parents may validly waive the child's physician–patient privilege; and whether parents can make a wide variety of decisions about the release of information to third parties. The answers to these questions will depend in part on whether or not the minor is an adolescent.

Young Minors

With very young patients, the psychiatrist is probably justified in treating the parents as the legal decision makers in almost all circumstances. Parents are generally empowered by statute to exercise a right of access and to waive the physician-patient privilege for minors (102). It is also appropriate to keep parents informed of the progress of treatment. This does not mean they are entitled to know everything their child has said in therapy. Particular caution should be exercised when disclosures might exacerbate problems in the family relationship. In addition, a psychiatrist is probably legally justified in releasing information to third parties when a parent consents. However, releasing very sensitive or embarrassing material on the parent's consent may not be consistent with a psychiatrist's ethical obligations.

An exception to these rules clearly exists where there is a possibility of child abuse. Most states require that child abuse be reported to the responsible agency, and fully immunize the doctor making the report. A child-abuse report can thus be a safe way for the psychiatrist to gain protection for a minor patient without risking a lawsuit claiming breach of confidentiality.

When a psychiatrist is releasing the medical records of a young minor, or testifying about the treatment of that child, the consent of one parent is generally sufficient. Sometimes, however, particularly in divorce proceedings or custody cases, two custodial parents may disagree about the decision to waive the right of confidentiality. In the context of ongoing litigation, it is advisable in this situation to withhold confidential information until the court rules on the validity of the purported waiver. If that is not possible, the psychiatrist should check the specific requirements of state law with an attorney.

Unfortunately, there usually is no clear line as to who is a very young minor for these purposes. Mental health confidentiality statutes generally address the issue (103). If there is no relevant statute, the psychiatrist is probably safe in relying on the parent's consent for any child under 12. This age is suggested in the APA's "Model Law on Confidentiality of Health and Social Service Records."

Adolescents

The rather simple rules applicable to very young minors begin to break down when a psychiatrist treats older children. It cannot be assumed that parents retain the same degree of control in the area of confidentiality when their children are adolescents.

It is reasonably clear that minors begin to possess an independent right to privacy at the point at which they are legally able to consent independently to medical care. Some state statutes explicitly provide that minors who are authorized to consent to their own treatment also have the right to control the release of information about that treatment. Even in the absence of such a clear statutory connection, there is probably little risk involved in releasing information on the consent of a minor who has legally consented to his or her own treatment. It would clearly be unwise for the psychiatrist to rely on the consent of the parent alone in such situations.

Unfortunately, according older minors the right to make decisions about confidentiality only when they have a right to consent to medical treatment will not fully discharge a psychiatrist's legal and ethical obligations. An adolescent's confidentiality interests must be considered even when they have no consent rights. As with adults, confidentiality is essential to treatment. Therefore, as a general rule, unless there are strong countervailing considerations, adolescents should be accorded the same confidentiality rights as adults. Psychiatrists frequently are most reluctant to observe this rule when it is a question of withholding information from parents. But this is the very confidentiality adolescents probably care most about. Not ensuring it may seriously interfere with treatment.

However, this general rule does not apply if disclosures are necessary to protect the minor from serious injuries or health hazards. When the competing intersts involved are not this serious, the psychiatrist may be able to find some other method to accomodate them. For example, minors may be persuaded to make disclosures to their parents themselves or to authorize the psychiatrist to do so. Or the psychiatrist may speak to the parents about the risks generally entailed in a particular course of action they have been following.

These same general rules should be followed in deciding what disclosures may be made to third parties. Special care should be taken when the disclosures are to benefit someone other than the patient, such as the psychiatrist. In such circumstances, it would be advisable for the psychiatrist to get the consent of both the patient and the patient's parents.

CONFIDENTIALITY AND AUTHORIZATION TO RELEASE INFORMATION

A valid, informed authorization to release information will protect a psychiatrist legally and ethically (104). To secure this protection, a psychiatrist should make certain that state law authorization requirements are satisfied and that the authorization actually covers the disclosures in question. Mental health confidentiality statutes generally specify the form for a valid authorization (105). Such statutes may also forbid the disclosure of information regardless of the patient's consent (106).

Mental health statutes usually require a signed authorization. Even when there is no such requirement, use of a consent form is generally advisable. A form is likely to make the patient focus on the process and the waiver of rights involved. In addition, if kept in the patient's record, it will corroborate the fact and extent of consent.

Psychiatrists should also satisfy themselves that the patient's consent is informed. The APA's ethical principles provide: "The continuing duty of the psychiatrist to protect the patient includes fully apprising him/her of the connotations of "waiving the privilege of privacy" (107). A psychiatrist requesting consent from a patient should make certain that the patient understands what he or she has consented to—the kind of information sought and the kind of material in his or her record, such as information from family members and other third parties. When consent has been obtained by a third party seeking the information and the psychiatrist is concerned that the patient would not have consented if aware of the kind of material involved or is not satisfied that the signature is valid or that the patient was aware that the request and authorization would be sent to the psychiatrist (as opposed to other providers), the psychiatrist should contact the patient and discuss these matters. This may be necessary when the consent was given rather routinely—as when the patient requests third-party reimbursement—and the party holding the consent asks for more than routine information.

Psychiatrists frequently infer consent to disclose information to a third party when they see patients for purposes of evaluation required by the third party in question (e.g., a potential employer, a court, or the military). This reliance is inadvisable. Although it may be obvious to the psychiatrist that disclosure to the third party is inherent in the very purpose of the examination, it may not be clear to the patient, who may assume he or she has the right to see the report and consent to its release. The patient is particularly likely to be angry if the report undercuts his or her interests. Therefore, at the beginning of the session the psychiatrist should explain the purpose of the examination and that the normal rules of confidentiality will not apply. This should be done in terms that the patient will understand and a notation of the explanation made in the psychiatrist's records. If the patient goes ahead with the examination, consent to the disclosure may be assumed.

This procedure is advisable for ethical, as well as legal, reasons. The APA's ethical principles provide:

> Psychiatrists are often asked to examine individuals for security purposes, to determine suitability for various jobs, and to determine legal competence. The psychiatrist must fully describe the nature and purpose and lack of confidentiality of the examination to the examinee at the beginning of the examination (108).

Even when a patient provides a blanket consent, psychiatrists should exercise discretion in what they disclose:

Ethically the psychiatrist must disclose only that information which is relevant to a given situation. He/she should avoid offering speculations as fact. Sensitive information such as an individual's sexual orientation or fantasy material is usually unnecessary (109).

If asked for information that is within the consent but which the psychiatrist feels the third party does not need, psychiatrists should consider contacting the party requesting the information to see if the party's interests can be accommodated without disclosing the sensitive information or records requested.

3

Psychiatric Records

G ood patient records can perform a number of functions for the psychiatrist in private practice. They clearly promote continuity of treatment. When a patient returns to treatment after a lapse of time, a record will enable a psychiatrist to familiarize himself or herself with the patient's background and prior course of treatment. A record may also advance treatment with a subsequent psychiatrist or provider. This will be especially important when a psychiatrist retires or moves away and is not available for personal consultations.

Properly kept records will also help a psychiatrist substantiate charges in the event of a dispute over a bill. For this purpose, a record should note each time a patient is seen and for what service or length of time. This practice should be followed for inpatient, as well as outpatient, services. Aggregating short inpatient visits and recording them as standard 45- or 50-minute sessions may precipitate challenges by third-party payors.

In addition, another important function of patient records may be to protect the psychiatrist in the event of a lawsuit. To serve this purpose, a record should first provide contemporaneous documentation of what actually occurred—what course of treatment was followed, at what intervals medication was prescribed or administered, what consents and authorizations were obtained, what instructions or warnings were given, etc. Judges and juries are likely to accept that what is recorded actually occurred—and that what is not recorded did not occur. This argues for more, rather than less, complete records. For example, a psychiatrist should record not only what medication was prescribed, but also the dosage and size of the prescription, details of the informed consent process, instructions given the patient (including the instruction that the patient inform the psychiatrist of side effects), the patient's known medication allergies and sensitivities, and notations of follow-ups on the effectiveness and side effects of the medication.

Most importantly, good records should explain significant treatment and patient-management decisions. Such a contemporaneous explanation is more likely to be accepted than what may appear to be an after-the-fact rationalization of unfortunate results. For each significant decision the record should reflect what the choice is expected to accomplish, why the psychiatrist believes it will be effective, what risks it involves and why they are justified, what alternative treatments were considered, why they were rejected, and what steps were taken to improve the effectiveness of the chosen treatment. For example, if a psychiatrist is treating a patient who presents a risk of suicide, the records should contain an assessment of the risk, the options considered for treatment and preventing suicide, their advantages and disadvantages, the psychiatrist's reasons for choosing or rejecting the options, and any special precautions taken by the psychiatrist to prevent the suicide (e.g., informing a patient's parents or roommates of the risk, giving the patient the psychiatrist's home phone number or the number of the emergency room). Other important decisions (e.g., commitment decisions, medication decisions, and decisions about whether the patient is dangerous and who should be warned) should be documented in a similar manner. The record should also reflect subsequent reviews of the initial decision for effectiveness and potential modifications.

This kind of record should provide significant protection to a psychiatrist in a malpractice action. The fact that a treatment decision turns out to be wrong (i.e., have negative results) does not mean that the psychiatrist has committed malpractice. He or she will be liable only if it is shown that customary care and judgment were not exercised in arriving at a decision. A record that clearly explains treatment decisions and documents the decision-making process should be very helpful in countering any such allegations.

Case law confirms the importance of records in this regard. For example, in *Abille v. United States* (110), a psychiatrist was held liable when a patient whose status he had downgraded from one appropriate for suicidal patients committed suicide. At the time of the change in status, the psychiatrist, contrary to his usual practice, had made no notes explaining his decision. The court acknowledged that a reasonable psychiatrist could have decided to change the patient's status but said that without notes there was reason for concern (111).

Many psychiatrists recognize the potential benefits of keeping thorough patient records but are concerned that such records will compromise their patients' rights of confidentiality. In most circumstances this concern is misplaced.

To begin with, documenting steps taken by the psychiatrist generally reveals relatively little about confidential information provided by the patient. In addition, except for search warrants, which are not generally used or available, a psychiatrist may be compelled to turn over records only by subpoena, when appropriate privilege claims can be raised. On the other hand, a psychiatrist may be questioned orally about a patient and the patient's treatment whenever the psychiatrist's records are susceptible to subpoena. Thus, the same information can usually be obtained from the psychiatrist directly as from the records. It is possible, however, that a psychiatrist will not be asked about his or her speculations on the patient's fantasies at a trial or deposition if they are not included in the records. Thus, unless absolutely necessary for conducting the treatment, such information should be excluded from a patient's record. Excluding such information is particularly advisable in those states which give patients access to their own records.

MAINTAINING RECORDS

In deciding whether to keep a record and how extensive it should be, psychiatrists should also consult state law. A number of states affirmatively require physicians to make a record for each patient and to keep it for a specified period of time. These requirements are generally contained in state administrative codes (112).

Because of the important function records can serve in litigation, they should be kept at least until the relevant statutes of limitations—the length of time a legal action may be brought—have elapsed. This is set by statute in each state. In many states the statute of limitations for malpractice is two or three years from the last treatment provided (113), and for breach of contract, six years.

Before making a decision about destroying old records, a psychiatrist should determine whether there are exceptions in the statute or case law that extend the basic statutory period. For example, the statute is usually tolled (i.e., stopped from running) during periods of a patient's incompetence. State provisions vary greatly as to length of the statutory period after the patient regains competence. The statute is also usually tolled while the patient is a minor.

Furthermore, in a number of states, the statute or decisional law provides that the statutory period does not begin to run until the patient knew or should have known that the damage occurred and was caused by the treatment. Fraud or conceal-ment on the part of the provider may also extend the statutory period. For these reasons, both lawyers and practitioners frequently advise that at least "basic" medical records be kept indefinitely (114).

Occasionally psychiatrists inquire about destroying a par-ticular patient's record (as opposed to setting a policy for the routine destruction of inactive records). There are two relevant considerations. First, the psychiatrist should determine whether state law forbids the destruction of documents with the intention of making them unavailable in a judicial proceed-ing, and, if so, at what point destruction is forbidden. Second, if a psychiatrist is forced to disclose during a judicial procedure that he or she destroyed the patient's record and that this action was not in accord with his or her usual policy, testimony and credibility are likely to be undercut. In short, selective destruction of records is not a good policy.

KEEPING RECORDS CONFIDENTIAL

Information from records obviously may be obtained without the psychiatrist's consent or knowledge. Therefore record-keeping, although it is not in itself inconsistent with confidentiality, imposes an obligation on the psychiatrist to take steps to protect against the unauthorized disclosure of confidential information. Records should be kept in a safe place that is accessible only to those who need access—the psychiatrist and staff members who may need the records to perform their duties. Although this may require special precautions in a group office, it should not be onerous. It may be more difficult to prevent unauthorized disclosures by office personnel with access to the records. Psychiatrists are held responsible for breaches of confidentiality by their employees. They must therefore impress on their staffs the importance of maintaining confidentiality and, if necessary, replace those employees who breach confidentiality or who do not observe office procedures in this regard.

Psychiatrists frequently ask whether confidentiality would be furthered by keeping two separate sets of records—progress notes (in which diagnosis, treatment decisions, and the progress of the patient are recorded) and personal notes (in which the psychiatrist could record impressions and speculations, very sensitive material, and information from third parties). The APA's "Model Law on Confidentiality of Health and Social Service" records recognizes this distinction. It would make three kinds of material not discoverable: 1) sensitive information received from third parties who asked that it be kept confidential; 2) information from patients that might hurt their relationships with others; and 3) the psychiatrist's speculations and impressions.

Unfortunately, only two jurisdictions have recognized such distinctions at the present time (115). To date, no judicial opinion has supported this distinction in ruling on the reach of a subpoena. Still, the distinction is defensible and may be analogous to the *work product* privilege that protects many lawyer's records. Thus, it may well be worth testing in a judicial proceeding. It is also possible that the distinction will be better received in a context other than private practice. For example, if notes are kept in one location, purely for research, with no indication of which patient they concern, an argument can be made that they are not "patient records."

PATIENT ACCESS TO RECORDS

Patients often demand either that their psychiatrist give them their own original records or that they be permitted access to their records. The actual records made and maintained by a psychiatrist in private practice belong to the psychiatrist and he or she is not obligated to relinquish them to a patient who demands them (116).

The rules governing patients' rights to inspect and copy their own medical records, however, are more complicated and vary substantially from jurisdiction to jurisdiction. In every state a patient can file suit against the physician alleging malpractice or other impropriety in the provision of professional services and subpoena the records for use in developing and proving his or her case. Moreover, an increasing number of states have enacted statutes authorizing patient access to medical records upon request and payment of administrative costs without resort to litigation.

These statutes vary as to the breadth of the right and the mechanism patients must follow to gain access. Some statutes give a right of access to the entire record, some to specified portions of a record, and others require only that a report or summary be provided. Access statutes frequently contain some limitation on patients' rights to inspect and copy their mental health records. Psychiatrists should familiarize themselves with these provisions. A common limitation is that which permits a psychiatrist or other mental health provider to withhold information that would have a negative impact on the patient's health. In some states this judgment may be made by the provider alone (although it presumably could be challenged by suit). In other states, the decision must be made, or reviewed, by an independent provider.

4

Billing and Payment Issues

From time to time almost all psychiatrists in private practice are faced with the problem of collecting unpaid bills. When usual collection methods (billing the patient, calling about the account, etc.) are exhausted, most use a local collection agency or attorney. Small claims court may be another option in appropriate circumstances.

Most collection agencies operate on a contingency-fee basis. The average commission charged is now around 40 percent (117), although this figure may vary substantially with the locale. Unfortunately, the average rate of recovery of such agencies is relatively low; in 1982, they recovered an average of 28 percent of all medical bills referred to them (118). Because of confidentiality and other ethical considerations, which will be discussed below, psychiatrists should take the time to find a reputable collection agency that will not harass patients or use other abusive collection tactics. An agency's affiliation with a national or statewide certified association and its good standing with that organization may provide some assurance of this. The easiest way to locate an agency that is reliable and will suit the needs of a psychiatric practice is probably to ask other local psychiatrists what agency they have found to be satisfactory.

Consulting other psychiatrists may also be helpful in finding a local attorney to pursue collection. Attorneys frequently charge on a fee-for-service, rather than a contingency, basis for collection work. Therefore, if the outstanding bill is small, attorneys' fees and litigation costs may well exceed potential recovery.

Hiring an attorney to institute suit may also be inadvisable in other circumstances. For example, if a psychiatrist is aware that the patient is very displeased with the services received, the psychiatrist should be cautious about instituting suit. Such an action may trigger a retaliatory malpractice claim that a patient might not otherwise have brought. Such a suit will be burdensome even when the psychiatrist is confident there is no basis for recovery. A suit is also not indicated if the chances of recovery are small because the patient has limited financial resources or a strong defense.

The costs of hiring an attorney for collection may make a small claims court a more attractive option. Because a psychiatrist will need to take over or assist in the preparation and presentation of such a case, using a small claims court will necessarily entail more of the psychiatrist's own time. Ground rules for the use of these courts vary from jurisdiction to jurisdiction and will substantially affect their utility as a collection tool. To begin with, the size of the maximum claim that may be brought varies substantially, with limits between $500 and $1500 the most common. In addition, many jurisdictions limit the number of times a particular plaintiff may sue in the court. A limit of three or four suits per calendar year is common.

A number of jurisdictions now limit the potential impact of a small claims verdict by providing that in such cases the losing party may seek review through a new trial and jury determination in the regular court system. A local attorney or the clerk of the small claims court should be able to answer any questions a psychiatrist may have about the procedure, advantages, and disadvantages of a small claims court.

LIMITATIONS ON COLLECTION METHODS

There are legal and ethical limitations on the collection methods a psychiatrist may use regardless of the patient's breach of
the treatment contract by nonpayment. First, a psychiatrist
must be careful to maintain the confidentiality of the relationship to the greatest extent possible. Many patients will not
want a psychiatrist to reveal that they are patients and will
consider such a disclosure in a court proceeding or to a
collection agency to be a breach of confidentiality. Other
collection methods should therefore be tried first. This will
also enable the patient to explain any extenuating circumstances causing tardiness in payment. If customary methods
are not effective, a psychiatrist should advise a patient that it
will be necesary to bring suit or refer an account for collection
if the bill remains unpaid or a collection schedule is not
arranged and followed.

If it becomes necessary to sue or to use an agency, a
psychiatrist should reveal only necessary information. The
patient's name and the amount of money owed should usually
suffice. If an itemized bill is required, services should be
described by a term such as *office visit* rather than by type of
therapy.

Although following these general guidelines should discharge a psychiatrist's legal and ethical obligations, a few
states have enacted statutes that set forth specifically what
steps a psychiatrist must take before referring an account to a
collection agency and what information may be revealed when
he or she does so. Psychiatrists considering using a collection
agency should check to see if any such requirements are
imposed by state law.

Psychiatrists must also make certain that their collection
methods—or those used on their behalf—do not constitute
harassment. Among the practices forbidden by law in various
jurisdictions are threats of criminal prosecution, disclosure or
threat of disclosure of false information calculated to affect a
credit reputation, contacting the debtor's employer before
obtaining a judgment, disclosure of information about the
debt without a legitimate need, abusing or harassing the
debtor, or using abusive language. A creditor who engages in

such practices may be liable for damages, including damages for emotional stress. Even if such practices are not specifically forbidden by state law, they may form the basis of an ethical complaint.

Finally, psychiatrists must make certain that they do not withhold services they are legally or ethically required to provide in order to encourage payment. Nonpayment will not be an adequate defense to such charges. For example, the AMA's ethical opinions provide the following:

> A physician who formerly treated a patient should not refuse for any reason to make his records of that patient promptly available on request to another physician presently treating the patient. . . . Medical reports should not be withheld because of an unpaid bill for medical services (119).

FACILITATING COLLECTION

If the person receiving treatment is to be responsible for payment, there is generally no need for him or her to execute a written agreement to pay. Under law an agreement is implied by the patient's willing recipience of services for which a provider reasonably expects payment. However, when a person other than the patient undertakes to pay for treatment, the provider may want to obtain a signed statement setting out the person's agreement to pay and the relevant terms. Such a statement should facilitate collection from a nonpatient. The person will be less likely to deny responsibility and, if recourse to the courts proves necessary, it will be easy for the provider to establish the agreement and its terms.

BILLING FOR MISSED SESSIONS AND
TREATMENT-RELATED SERVICES

Psychiatric services, like other services, are provided pursuant to a contract—even though in some instances the contract is not in writing. A psychiatrist is generally free to bill the patient at the rates and for the services he or she has established in advance. Thus, billing for missed appointments is usually appropriate as long as the patient has been advised at the outset of treatment that this will be the psychiatrist's practice. The APA's ethical guidelines provide the following:

> It is ethical for the psychiatrist to make a charge for a missed appointment when this falls within the terms of the specific contractual agreement with the patient. Charging for a missed appointment or for one not cancelled 24 hours in advance need not, in itself, be considered unethical if a patient is fully advised that the physician will make such a charge. The practice, however, should be resorted to infrequently and always with the utmost consideration of the patient and his/her circumstances (120).

Although the patient may be charged for missed sessions, a psychiatrist should not represent to a third-party payor that treatment was provided during a missed session. Many such payors will cover only medically necessary services that have actually been rendered. Thus, billing of an insuror for missed appointments could be deemed misrepresentation and lead to insuror complaints.

This same general rule applies to billing for most extras and incidental services that psychiatrists may be asked to provide—telephone conversations with patients, preparing accident reports, filling out complex insurance forms, etc. (121). To avoid disputes and consequent problems in the treatment relationship with the patient, the psychiatrist should discuss his or her charge for the service in question as soon as requested to provide it. Whether such services are covered by third-party payors will depend on the terms of the patient's insurance policy.

CHARGING INTEREST

The American Medical Association has decided that interest may be charged on overdue accounts so long as patients are properly informed. A 1982 revision of an earlier opinion by the Judicial Council provides that it is permissible to charge interest as long as the patient is notified of this practice in advance. However, when credit is extended in this way, it is necessary to comply with the requirements of the Federal Truth-in-Lending Act and any applicable state law. These laws mandate detailed and extensive disclosures on each bill, specifying size of type, placement, and prominence of the provisions. The complexity of these requirements and the potential for civil liability and criminal penalties make assistance of counsel essential for the professional who wishes to charge interest. A local attorney should be able to develop a billing form and instructions that will facilitate compliance with both federal and state law.

Notes

1. See, e.g., Fishalow, *The Tort Liability of the Psychiatrist*, 4 Bulletin of the American Academy of Psychiatry and Law 191, 192 (1975); Rosenblatt and Leroy, *Avoiding Psychiatric Liability*, 9 Cal West L Rev 260, 261(1973); Halleck, *Law in the Practice of Psychiatry* (1980), 20; Gutheil and Appelbaum, *Clinical Handbook of Psychiatry and the Law* (1982).

2. It has been estimated that only about 1.5 claims are filed per 100 psychiatrists each year compared to five claims per 100 physicians generally. Dawidoff, *The Malpractice of Psychiatrists: Malpractice in Psychoanalysis, Psychotherapy, and Psychiatry* (1973); Slawson, *Psychiatric Malpractice: A Regional Incidence Study*, 126 Am J Psychiatry 1302 (1970).

3. Slawson, "Psychiatric Malpractice: A California State-wide Survey," Bulletin of the American Academy of Psychiatry and the Law, 6(1978) 58–63.

4. In determining standard practice, courts traditionally looked only at the practice in the defendant's locality. Many courts have now abandoned this rule, judging

physicians by a national standard. In addition, many states that now apply the locality rule for general practitioners hold specialists (such as psychiatrists) to a national standard.

5. See W. Prosser, *Handbook on the Law of Torts.*

6. An English case, *Landau v. Werner,* 105 Sol. J. 257, 105 Sol. J. 1008(1961) is the only reported case that approaches finding liability for negligent psychotherapy. Even this case was based on the doctor's actions after termination of psychotherapy. Concerned about the effects of abrupt cessation by the patient who believed she had fallen in love with him, the psychiatrist initiated several social contacts with the patient. The patient was upset by these, her condition deteriorated, and she sued.

7. See, e.g., *Eisele v. Malone,* 2 App. Div. 2d 550, 157 N.Y.S.2d 155 (1956); *Stone v. Proctor,* 259 N.C. 633, 131 S.E.2d 297 (1963); *Collins v. Hand,* 431 Pa. 378, 246 A.2d 398 (1968).

8. See, e.g., *Brown v. Moore,* 247 F.2d 711 (3d Cir. 1957), *cert. den.,* 355 U.S. 882 (1957); *Quick v. Benedictine Sisters Hospital Ass'n,* 257 Minn 470, 102 N.W.2d 39 (1960), *Adams v. State,* 71 Wash. 2d 414, 429 P.2d 109 (1967).

9. A limited number of psychatrists have argued that sexual relationships with patients may be therapeutic. See, e.g., Shepard, *The Love Treatment: Sexual Intimacy Between Patients and Psychotherapists* (1970); McCartney, *Overt Transference,* 2 J Sex Research 227 (1966).

10. See Halleck, *supra,* 102; Sadoff, *Legal Issues in the Care of Psychiatric Patients* (1982) 68.

11. American Psychiatric Association, *The Principles of Medical Ethics with Annotations Especially Applicable to Psychiatry* (hereinafter, APA *Principles),* Section 2, Annotation 1.

12. Psychiatrists also risk losing their licenses if they have sex with their patients. See, e.g., *Bernstein v. Board of Medical Examiners,* 204 Cal. App. 2d 378, 22 Cal. Rptr. 419 (1962); *Shepherd v. Ambach,* 414 H.S.Y.2d 817 (1979).

13. The study found that defendants won in fewer than 30 percent of these cases. Hogan, *The Regulation of Psychotherapists, Volume III, A Review of Malpractice Suits in the United States* (1979) 12.

14. See, e.g., *Roy v. Hartogs*, 8l Misc. 2d 350, 366 N.Y.S.2d 297 (Cir. Ct. N.Y. Final Term 1979); *Zupkin v. Freeman*, 436 S.W.2d 753 (Mo. 1968).

15. See, e.g., *Roy v. Hartogs*, 81 Misc. 2d 350, 366 N.Y.S.2d 292 (N.Y. Civ. Ct., 1975).

16. The argument was rejected in a different context in *Whitesell v. Green*, No. 38745 (Hawaii Dist. Ct., November 19, l973). Plaintiff and his wife had consulted a psychologist for marital counseling. Two weeks after the end of counseling, the psychologist and the wife began a sexual relationship. The plaintiff claimed breach of duty; the psychologist argued that there was no professional relationship at the time of the affair. Plaintiff was awarded $18,000 in damages.

17. American Psychiatric Association, *Opinions of the Ethics Committee on the Principles of Medical Ethics* (hereinafter, APA *Opinions*), Section 2-D (1983).

18. The number of reported decisions involving drug therapy have increased steadily in recent years. Hogan, *supra*, at 381.

19. *Clinical Psychiatry News*, October, 1983, 1.

20. See, e.g., *Christy v. Saliterman*, 288 Minn. 144, 179 N.W.2d 288 (1970) (plaintiff successfully argued that the psychiatrist should have recognized that a particular drug would have undesirable side effects); *Rosenfield v. Coleman*, 19 Pa. D. & C. 635 (1959) (court found psychiatrist's prescription of addictive drug to patient in effort to help him understand that he had addictive personality was beyond professional norms).

21. See, e.g., *Runyon v. Reid*, 510 P.2d 943 (Okla. 1973); *Rouse v. Twin Pines Sanitarium*, 162 Cal. App. 2d 639, 328 P.2d 536 (1958).

22. See, e.g., *Runyon v. Reid, supra.*

23. Schwartz, *Liability for Causing Suicide: A Synthesis of Law and Psychiatry*, 24 Vanderbilt L. Rev. 217.

24. See *Clites v. Iowa*, 322 N.W.2d 917 (Iowa Ct. App. 1981), which involved both informed consent and proper administration of psychotic drugs. The plaintiff, a mentally retarded man, had been admitted to a state facility at the age of 11. Between the ages of 18 and 23, major tranquilizers had been prescribed to control his aggressive behavior. At 23, tardive dyskinesia was diagnosed. The plaintiff sued, claiming that defendants had prescribed tranquilizers negligently and that they had not obtained informed consent. The Iowa Court of Appeals affirmed the damage award of $760,165. The test of negligence, according to the court, was whether defendants had adhered to "industry" standards. It found the following to be deviations from those standards: failure to provide regular tests and physical exams; failure to provide drug holidays; failure to act when the first signs of tardive dyskinesia became apparent; the use of several drugs in a combination inappropriate in light of the patient's status and the types of medications used; use of tranquilizers for purposes of convenience rather than therapy; and failure to obtain consent.

25. See APA, *American Psychiatric Association Task Force Report 18: Tardive Dyskinesia* 123 (1980) 27–45; Applebaum and Gutheil, *Drug Refusal: A Study of Psychiatric Inpatients*, 137 Am J Psychiatry 330, 333–34 (1980).

26. APA *Task Force Report 18, supra*, at 43–44, 171.

27. AMA ethical opinion 6.03 provides in part, "Physicians are free to choose whom they will serve. . . ." AMA's *Current Opinions of the Judicial Council* (hereinafter, AMA *Opinions*).

28. Section 8.10 of the AMA's *Opinions* concludes, "...once having undertaken a case, the physician should not neglect the patient, nor withdraw from the case without giving sufficient notice to the patient, the relatives or responsible friends sufficiently long in advance of with-

drawal to permit another medical attendant to be secured."

29. APA *Opinions*, Section 6-C.

30. *Restatement of Torts (Second)* § 315 (1965).

31. 17 Cal. 3d 425, 551 P.2d 334 (1976).

32. 27 Cal. 3d 741, 614 P.2d 728 (1980).

33. In *Thompson*, parents of a boy murdered by a juvenile offender within 24 hours of his release sued the county. Neighborhood residents had not been warned despite the fact that the offender was known to have violent tendencies towards children and had "indicated that he would, if released, take the life of a young child residing in the neighborhood." He had not said which, if any, child was his target. The court found no duty to warn the police, the public, or the offender's mother because the victim was not identifiable.

34. 168 N.J. Super. 466, 403 A.2d 500 (1979).

35. *Chrite v. United States*, No. 81-83944, _____ F.Supp. _____ (E.D Mich., May 26, 1983); *Davis v. Yong Oh-Lhim*, No. 59284 (Mich. Ct. App., March 1, 1983); *Durflinger v. Artiles*, No. 75-63-C6 (D. Kan. 1981). *See also Jablonski v. United States*, _____ F.2d _____ (9th Cir. 1983).

36. *Cairl v. State*, 323 N.W.2d 20 (Minn. 1982); *Heltsley v. Votteler*, 327 N.W.2d 759 (Ia. 1982); *Leedy v. Hartnett*, 510 F.Supp. 1125 (M.D. Pa. 1981); *Brady v. Hopper*, Civ. No. 83-JM-451 (D. Colo. Sept. 14, 1983); *Furr v. Spring Grove State Hospital* (Md. Ct. Spec. App. Jan. 7, 1983); *Doyle v. United States*, 530 F.Supp. 1278 (C.D. Cal. 1982).

37. See, respectively, *Bellah v. Greenson*, 141 Cal. Rptr. 92 (Cal. App. 1977) and *Cole v. Taylor*, 301 N.W.2d 766 (Ia. 1981). To date, these are the only courts that have ruled on these issues.

38. *See also, Cairl v. State, supra.*

39. *See also, Davis v. Yong Oh-Lhim, supra.*

40. 130 P.H.L.J. 107 (Pa. Ct. Com. Pl. 1981).

41. 415 A.2d 625 (Md. Ct. Spec. App. 1980).

42. 497 F.Supp. 185 (D. Neb. 1980).

43. *Leverett v. Ohio*, 61 Ohio App. 2d 35, 399 N.E.2d 106 (1978); *Bradley Center, Inc. v. Wessner*, 296 S.E.2d 693 (Ga. 1982); *Johnson v. United States*, 409 F.Supp. 1283 (M.D. Fla. 1976).

44. No. 49490-8 (Wash. Oct. 20, 1983).

45. The Court's finding that the victim was foreseeable was dependent on the lower court's finding the failure to obtain the patient's former medical records (which would have confirmed his dangerousness) to be a separate act of malpractice. In upholding this finding, the Court of Appeals discussed neither the problem of discovering where the patient had received treatment (the patient refused to state), nor the patient's right of confidentiality, which might have prevented access to the records.

46. *Clinical Psychiatry News*, October, 1983, 1.

47. In these suits, the hospital and hospital personnel are also frequently named as defendants.

48. See, e.g., Murphy, *Clinical Identification of Suicidal Risk*, 27 Arch. Gen. Psychiat. 356 (1972); Motto, *Suicide Prevention in Medical Practice*, 210 JAMA (1969); Murphy, *Recognition of Suicidal Risk*, 62 So. Med. J. 723 (1967); American Psychiatric Association Task Force Report 8: *Clinical Aspects of the Violent Individual* (1974).

49. See, e.g., *White v. United States*, 244 F.Supp. 127 (E.D. Va. 1965), *aff'd*, 359 F.2d 989 (9th Cir. 1966); *Baker v. United States*, 226 F.Supp. 129 (S.D. Iowa 1969), *aff'd*, 343 F.2d 222 (8th Cir. 1965); *Fernandez v. Baruch*, 52 N.J. 127, 244 A.2d 109 (1968).

50. *Meier v. Ross General Hospital*, 69 Cal. 2d 420, 71 Cal Rptr. 903, 445 P.2d 519 (1968).

51. *Farrow v. Health Serv. Corp.*, 604 P.2d 474 (Utah 1979).

52. Several courts have recognized, however, that a determined patient may commit suicide despite all precautions. See *Skar v. City of Lincoln, Nebraska*, 599 F.2d 253 (8th Cir. 1975); *Dahlberg v. Jones*, 232 Wis. 6, 285 N.W. 841 (1939).

53. See, e.g., *Topel v. Long Island Jewish Medical Center*, 55 N.Y.2d 682, 466 N.Y.S.2d 293, 431 N.E.2d 293 (1981). Reversing a jury verdict in plaintiff's favor, the New York Court of Appeals said, "[The patient's] reaction to constant surveillance, the possibility that his heart condition would be aggravated by continuing such surveillance, the gesture-like nature of his prior suicidal indications, the rehabilitative aspects of 'open-ward' treatment and the enhanced probability of obtaining [the patient's] consent to electroshock therapy in the more relaxed open ward atmosphere were all factors which defendant doctor could properly consider in reaching the judgment whether, on balance, the prescribed program was worth the risk involved." See also *Dillman v. Hellman*, 283 So.2d 388 (Fla. App. 1973); *Baker v. United States*, 226 F.Supp. 129 (S.D. Iowa 1964) *aff'd*, 343 F.2d 222 (8th Cir. 1965); *Schwartz v. United States*, 226 F.Supp. (D.D.C. 1964).

54. See, e.g., *Weatherly v. United States*, 109 Misc. 2d 1024, 441 N.Y.S.2d 319 (Ct. Cl. 1981); *Abille v. United States*, 482 F.Supp. 703 (N.D. Cal. 1980).

55. 409 F.Supp. 1283 (M.D. Fla. 1981).

56. 80 App. Div. 2d 821, 437 N.Y.S.2d 321 (1981).

57. See also *Taig v. State of New York*, 19 App. Div. 2d 182, 241 N.Y.S.2d 495 (1963); *Centero v City of New York*, 48 App. Div. 2d 812, 369 N.Y.S.2d 710, *aff'd* 40 N.Y.2d 932, 389 N.Y.S.2d 837.

58. See, e.g., *Bell v. New York City Health and Hospitals Corp.*, 90 App. Div. 2d 270, 456 N.Y.S.2d 787 (1982).

59. 512 F.Supp. 670 (N.D. Tex. 1981).

60. See also *Runyon v. Reid*, 570 P.2d 943 (Okla. 1973).

61. The absence of such a record seems largely responsible for the verdict against the psychiatrist in *Abille v. United States*, 482 F.Supp. 703 (N.D.Cal. 1980). The court conceded that a reasonable psychiatrist might have decided that a patient could be reclassified from a suicide to a less dangerous status but said that without notes there was reason for concern that the decision had been negligently made.

62. See, e.g., *Getchell v. Mansfield*, 250 Or. 174, 489 P.2d 953 (Or. 1971).

63. 148 N.J. Super. 168, 372 A.2d 360 (1977).

64. This generally involves petitioning the proper court for a declaration that the patient is incompetent and for appointment of a guardian. In most states the court may appoint either a general guardian or a limited guardian, with power to make specified decisions, such as treatment decisions. In some circumstances, after finding the patient incompetent the judge will also make the treatment decision.

65. See, e.g., *Anonymous v. State*, 236 N.Y.S.2d 88 (App. Div. 1963); *Farber v. Olkon*, 254 P.2d 520 (Cal. 1953).

66. Principle IV of the American Medical Association's *Principles of Medical Ethics* provides, "A physician shall respect the rights of patients, of colleagues, and of other health professionals, and shall safeguard patient confidences within the constraints of the law."

67. APA *Principles*, Section 4, Annotation 1.

68. *Clinical Psychiatry News, supra.*

69. Occasionally statutes will specifically cover such staff. See, e.g., N.Y. Civ. Prac. Law, § 4504.

70. See, e.g., *Staat v. Staat*, 291 Minn. 394, 192 N.W.2d 192 (1971). But see *Weis v. Weis*, 147 Ohio St. 416, 72 N.E.2d 245 (1947).

71. This is true even where the statute refers only to "communications." See e.g., *State v. District Court*, 218 N.W.2d 641 (1974).

72. See, e.g., *Furguson v. Quaker City Life Insurance Company*, 129 A.2d 189 (D.C. Minn. App. 1957).

73. See, e.g., Cal. Evid. Code § 992; *State v. Thomas* 275 P.2d 408 (Ariz. 1954).

74. See, e.g., Cal. Evid. Code § 992, *Ellis v. Ellis*, 472 S.W.2d 74 (Tenn. Sup. Ct. App. 1971).

75. See, e.g., *Grosslight v. Superior Court*, 140 Cal. Rptr. 278 (1977).

76. Md. Ct. App. (May 31, 1983).

77. For example, in California, minors 12 or older may consent to psychotherapy when they are mature and in serious need of treatment or have been the victims of incest or child abuse. Privilege decisions related to such treatment are to be made by the "professional person rendering such mental health treatment or health counselling." Cal. Evid. Code § 1014.5.

78. Some states require that a waiver be express or written. See, e.g., Md. Ct. & Jud. Proc. Ann. § 9-109(d)(4), Tex. Rev. Civ. Stat. Ann. Art. 5561h § 4(a)(2).

79. See, e.g., *Giamanco v. Giamanco*, 57 A.D.2d 564, 393 N.Y.S.2d 453 (1977).

80. See, e.g., *Mancinelli v. Texas Easten Transmission Corp.*, 34 A.D.2d 535, 308 N.Y.S.2d 882 (1970).

81. Compare, e.g., *Tylitzka v. Triple X Service Inc.*, 261 N.E.2d 533 (Ill. 1970) and *In Re Lifschutz*, 467 P.2d 557 (Cal. 1970).

82. See, e.g., *Hickox v. Hickox*, 410 N.Y.S.2d 81 (1978) and *Atwood v. Atwood*, 550 S.W.2d 465 (Ky. 1974).

83. See, e.g., N.Y. Civ. Prac. law § 4504(c).

84. See, e.g., Md. Cts. & Jud. Proc. Ann. § 9-109(3)(ii).

85. Mass. Gen. Laws Ann. Ch. 233 † 20B(e).

86. APA *Principles*, Section 4, Annotation 2.

87. See, e.g., *Horne v. Patton*, 291 Ala. 701, 287 So.2d 824 (1973); *Doe v. Roe*, 93 Misc. 2d 201, 400 N.Y.S.2d 668 (1977); *Hammonds v. Aetna Casualty & Surety Co.*, 243; *Quarles v. Sutherland*, 215 Tenn. 651, 389 S.W.2d 249 (1965); *Hague v. Williams*, 37 N.J.328, 181 A.2d 395 (1962).

88. See, e.g., *Horne v. Patton, supra; Doe v. Roe, supra; Hammonds v. Aetna Casualty & Surety Co., supra; Glenn v. Kirlin*, 248 So.2d 832 (La. Ct. App. 1971).

89. *Horne v. Patton, supra; Doe v. Roe, supra; Hammonds v. Aetna Casualty & Surety Co., supra; Glenn v. Kirlin*, 248 So.2d 832 (La. Ct. App. 1971).

90. See, e.g., *Horne v. Patton, supra; MacDonald v. Clinger* (N.Y. App. Div. 1983).

91. See, e.g., *Simonson v. Swenson*, 104 Neb. 224, 177 N.W. 831 (1920).

92. See, e.g., *Curry v. Corn*, 52 Misc. 2d 1035, 277 N.Y.S.2d 470; *Clark v. Geraci*, 29 Misc. 2d 791, 208 N.Y.S. 2d 564 (dictum); *Quarles v. Sutherland, supra.*

93. See, e.g., *Horne v. Patton, supra; Clark v. Geraci, supra; Hopewell v. Adebimpe, supra.*

94. See, e.g., *MacDonald v. Clinger, supra.*

95. See, e.g., *Hague v. Williams, supra; Hammond v. Aetna Cas. & Sur. Co., supra; Quarles v. Sutherland, supra.*

96. *Doe v. Roe, supra.*

97. APA *Principles*, Section 2, Annotation 4 provides in part, "A psychiatrist may release confidential information only with the authorization of the patient or under proper legal compulsion."

98. See, e.g., *Simonson v. Swenson, supra; Hofman v. Blackman*, 241 So.2d 752 (Fla. App. 1970) (patient suffering from contagious disease); *Schatter v. Spicer*, 295 N.W.2d 134 (S. Dak. 1974); *Berry v. Moench*, 8 Utah 2d 191, 331 P.2d 814

(1958) (physician justified in warning patient's girlfriend about patient's mental health).

99. See, e.g., Illinois Mental Health and Developmental Disability Confidentiality Act, Ch. 91-1/2, § 801, *et seq.*; District of Columbia Mental Health Information Act, D.C. Code Ann. 6-201, *et seq.*

100. APA *Opinions*, Section 4-K, provides the following:

Question: Can I give confidential information about a recently deceased mother to her grieving daughter?

Answer: No. Ethically, her confidences survive her death. Legally this is an unclear issue varying from one jurisdiction to another. Further, there is a risk of the information being used to seek an advantage in the contesting of a will or in competition with other surviving family members. (January 1983)

101. APA *Principles*, Section 4, Annotation 7.

102. But see exceptions discussed above.

103. For example, in Illinois, parents retain the right to consent to the disclosure of records and information of all minors under 12. Ill. Stat. Ann. Ch. 91-1/2, § 805. In the District of Columbia, a parent of a child under 14 may authorize disclosures. D.C. Code Ann. § 6-2015.

104. Text accompanying note 86, *supra*.

105. For example, in Illinois consent must be in writing and specify the purpose of the disclosure, the nature of the information disclosed, the right to inspect and copy the information, the period of time the consent is valid and the patient's right to revoke the consent. Ill. Stat. Ann. Ch. 91-1/2, § 805.

106. The District of Columbia Mental Health Information Act limits the information that may be disclosed to third-party payors to administrative information, diagnostic

information, the reason for continuing treatment, an estimation of the length of continued treatment, and the patient's voluntary or involuntary status.

107. APA *Principles*, Section 4, Annotation 2.

108. *Id.*, Section 4, Annotation 6.

109. *Id.*, Section 4, Annotation 5.

110. 482 F.Supp. 703 (N.D. Cal. 1980).

111. See also *Centeno v. City of New York*, 40 N.Y. 2d 932, 389 N.Y.S.2d 837, 358 N.E.2d 527 (1976).

112. For example, New York state regulations require a physician to "maintain a record for each patient which accurately reflects the evaluation and treatment of the patient." (N.Y.S. Bd. of Regents Rules § 29.2(a)(7)).

113. As discussed earlier, a suit for breach of confidentiality may be based on a breach of contract theory.

114. See, e.g., R.L. Sadoff, *Legal Issues in the Care of Psychiatric Patients* (1982), 18; H. Hassard, "Retention of Medical Records," The Western Journal of Medicine, March 1981, 1.

115. See Ill. Stat. Ann. Ch. 91-1/2; D.C. Code § 6-2003.

116. AMA *Opinions*, Section 7.02, provides in part, "Notes made in treating a patient are primarily for the physician's own use and constitute his personal property."

117. *Medical Economics*, Dec. 26, 1983, 37.

118. *Id.*

119. AMA *Opinions*, Section 7.01.

120. APA *Principles*, Section 2, Annotation 6.

121. Filling out standard insurance claims forms, however, is not considered to be an extra service for which the patient may be billed. AMA's *Current Opinions of the Judicial Council*, section 6.06 provides, "The attending physician

should complete without charge the appropriate 'simpli-
fied' insurance claim forms as part of his service to the
patient to enable the patient to receive his benefits. A
charge for more complex forms may be made in confor-
mity with local customs."

Appendix 1:
Additional Readings

In addition to the sources cited in the footnotes, the following books provide useful additional information and references:

Gutheil TG, Appelbaum PS: Clinical Handbook of Psychiatry and Law. New York, McGraw-Hill, 1982

Halleck SG: Law in the Practice of Psychiatry. New York, Plenum, 1980

Hofling CA (ed): Law and Ethics in the Practice of Psychiatry. New York, Brunner/Mazel, 1981

Sadoff RL: Legal Issues in the Care of Psychiatric Patients. New York, Springer, 1982

Simon RI: Psychiatric Intervention and Malpractice. Springfield, IL, Charles C Thomas, 1982

Stone AA: Law, Psychiatry, and Morality: Essays and Analysis. Washington, DC, American Psychiatric Press, 1984

Appendix 2: Model Forms

These forms are for general guidance only. Consult an attorney to ensure that there are no additional requirements in your jurisdiction.

Consent for Treatment with

_____
[Name of Medication]

I, _____, am a patient

of Dr. _____. Dr. _____
has informed me that he/she recommends that I receive

the medication _____ for the
treatment of my illness. He/she has informed me of the
nature of the treatment and has explained to me the risks

of possible side effects, including _____

_____ .
[He/she specifically discussed the risk of tardive dyskinesia, which may cause involuntary tic-like movements in the face, tongue, neck, arms, and/or legs].

I understand that although Dr. _____
has explained to me the most common side effects of this
treatment there may be other side effects, and that I

should promptly inform Dr. _____ or another member of the staff if there are any unexpected
changes in my condition.

I understand that I may not be compelled to take this
medication and that I may decide to stop taking it at any
time.

I also understand that although Dr. _____
believes that this medication will help me, there is no
guarantee as to the results that may be expected.

On this basis I authorize Dr. _____ or anyone authorized by him/her to administer _____
at such intervals as he/she deems advisable.

Signed _____

Dated _____

Witnessed: _____

Termination of Psychiatrist–Patient Relationship

[Date]

Dear [Name of Patient]:

This is to inform you that [psychiatrist may, but is not required to specify reason] I believe it is necessary to terminate our professional relationship.

I have been serving as your psychiatrist since [specify date], and am currently treating you for [indicate diagnosis] with a program of [specify treatment mode, including any drugs]. In my view, you [would/would not] benefit from continued treatment.

If you wish to continue to receive treatment, you are, of course, free to contact any psychiatrist of your choice. However, you may wish to contact one of the following [psychiatrists/facilities], who may be willing to accept you as a patient. [Indicate specific referrals.] If you find that none of these choices is acceptable, please contact me; I will make every effort to suggest additional alternatives. If you do decide to obtain treatment from one of these psychiatrists or facilities, or from any other psychiatrist or facility of your choice, I will be happy to forward your clinical records to your new doctor on your written authorization.

Finally be assured that I will be available to treat you until you have had a reasonable opportunity to seek treatment elsewhere. [The following factors, among others, may be used to determine what is "reasonable" in a particular situation: condition of the patient, length of the psychiatrist–patient relationship, availability of other psychiatric services in the community, reason for termination, and amount of money owed, if any.]

I have enclosed an extra copy of this letter, and would be grateful if you could sign and return it to me in order to ensure that you have in fact received the letter.

_____
[Psychiatrist's Name]

_____
[Patient's Name]

Patient Authorization for Release
of Medical Information

I, _____ , hereby authorize

Dr. _____ to release the information
in my medical records, including diagnoses, treatment

information, and other notations, to _____

_____ (physician, insurance company, etc.). I also

authorize Dr. _____ to discuss
my treatment if appropriate. This released information
may be used solely for the purpose of (medical treatment,
paying insurance and benefits, etc.). This authorization is

valid for the period _____ (months/years).

Signed: _____

Date: _____

Agreement to Pay
for Treatment of Relative

I, _____ , agree to pay

Dr. _____ for services provided

by him/her at my request to _____ ,

my _____ (relationship), at the following

rate: _____ .
    I understand that I am personally responsible for the

cost of services rendered by Dr. _____ .
    It is my intention that this agreement be enforceable in

the courts of the State of _____ .

Signed: _____

Date:　 _____

Witness: _____

Appendix 3:
The Principles of Medical Ethics with Annotations Especially Applicable to Psychiatry

1981 Edition
Revised

The Principles of Medical Ethics
With Annotations Especially
Applicable to Psychiatry

In 1973, the American Psychiatric Association published the first edition of the PRINCIPLES OF MEDICAL ETHICS WITH ANNOTATIONS ESPECIALLY APPLICABLE TO PSYCHIATRY. Subsequently, revisions were published as the Board of Trustees and the Assembly approved additional annotations. In July of 1980, the American Medical Association approved a new version of the Principles of Medical Ethics (the first revision since 1957) and the APA Ethics Committee[1] incorporated many of its annotations into the new Principles, which resulted in the 1981 edition and the Revision.

FOREWORD

ALL PHYSICIANS should practice in accordance with the medical code of ethics set forth in the Principles of Medical Ethics of the American Medical Association. An up-to-date expression and elaboration of these statements is found in the *Opinions and Reports of the Judicial Council* of the American Medical Association.[2] Psychiatrists are strongly advised to be familiar with these documents.[3]

However, these general guidelines have sometimes been difficult to interpret for psychiatry, so further annotations to the basic principles are offered in this document. While psychiatrists have the same goals as all physicians, there are special ethical problems in psychiatric practice that differ in coloring and degree from ethical problems in other branches of medical practice, even though the basic principles are the same. The annotations are not designed as absolutes and will be revised from time to time so as to be applicable to current practices and problems.

Following are the AMA Principles of Medical Ethics, printed in their entirety, and then each principle printed separately along with an annotation especially applicable to psychiatry.

---

[1]The committee included Herbert Klemmer, M.D., Chairperson, Miltiades Zaphiropoulos, M.D., Ewald Busse, M.D., John R. Saunders, M.D., Robert McDevitt, M.D., and J. Brand Brickman, M.D. William P. Camp, M.D., and Robert A. Moore, M.D., serve as consultants to the APA Ethics Committee.

[2]Opinions and Reports of the Judicial Council. Chicago, American Medical Association, 1981.

[3]Chapter 8, Section 1 of the By-Laws of the American Psychiatric Association states, "All members of the American Psychiatric Association shall be bound by the ethical code of the medical profession, specifically defined in the *Principles of Medical Ethics* of the American Medical Association." In interpreting the APA Constitution and By-Laws, it is the opinion of the Board of Trustees that inactive status in no way removes a physician member from responsibility to abide by the *Principles of Medical Ethics*.

PRINCIPLES OF MEDICAL ETHICS, AMERICAN MEDICAL ASSOCIATION

PREAMBLE

The medical profession has long subscribed to a body of ethical statements developed primarily for the benefit of the patient. As a member of this profession, a physician must recognize responsibility not only to patients, but also to society, to other health professionals, and to self. The following Principles, adopted by the American Medical Association, are not laws, but standards of conduct which define the essentials of honorable behavior for the physician.

SECTION 1

A physician shall be dedicated to providing competent medical service with compassion and respect for human dignity.

SECTION 2

A physician shall deal honestly with patients and colleagues, and strive to expose those physicians deficient in character or competence, or who engage in fraud or deception.

SECTION 3

A physician shall respect the law and also recognize a responsibility to seek changes in those requirements which are contrary to the best interests of the patient.

SECTION 4

A physician shall respect the rights of patients, of colleagues, and of other health professionals, and shall safeguard patient confidences within the constraints of the law.

SECTION 5

A physician shall continue to study, apply, and advance scientific knowledge, make relevant information available to patients, colleagues, and the public, obtain consultation, and use the talents of other health professionals when indicated.

SECTION 6

A physician shall, in the provision of appropriate patient care, except in emergencies, be free to choose whom to serve, with whom to associate, and the environment in which to provide medical services.

SECTION 7

A physician shall recognize a responsibility to participate in activities contributing to an improved community.

Principles with Annotations

Following are each of the AMA Principles of Medical Ethics printed separately along with annotations especially applicable to psychiatry.

PREAMBLE

The medical profession has long subscribed to a body of ethical statements developed primarily for the benefit of the patient. As a member of this profession, a physician must recognize responsibility not only to patients, but also to society, to other health professionals, and to self. The following Principles, adopted by the American Medical Association, are not laws, but standards of conduct which define the essentials of honorable behavior for the physician. [4]

SECTION 1

A physician shall be dedicated to providing competent medical service with compassion and respect for human dignity.

1. The patient may place his/her trust in his/her psychiatrist knowing that the psychiatrist's ethics and professional responsibilities preclude him/her gratifying his/her own needs by exploiting the patient. This becomes particularly important because of the essentially private, highly personal, and sometimes intensely emotional nature of the relationship established with the psychiatrist.

2. A psychiatrist should not be a party to any type of policy that excludes, segregates, or demeans the dignity of any patient because of ethnic origin, race, sex, creed, age, socioeconomic status, or sexual orientation.

3. In accord with the requirements of law and accepted medical practice, it is ethical for a physician to submit his/her work to peer review and to the ultimate authority of the medical staff executive body and the hospital administration and its governing body. In case of dispute, the ethical psychiatrist has the following steps available:

   a. Seek appeal from the medical staff decision to a joint conference committee, including members of the medical staff executive committee and the executive committee of the governing board. At this appeal, the ethical psychiatrist could request that outside opinions be considered.
   b. Appeal to the governing body itself.
   c. Appeal to state agencies regulating licensure of hospitals if, in the particular state, they concern themselves with matters of professional competency and quality of care.
   d. Attempt to educate colleagues through development of research projects and data and presentations at professional meetings and in professional journals.

---

[4]Statements in italics are taken directly from the American Medical Association's Principles of Medical Ethics.

e. Seek redress in local courts, perhaps through an enjoining injunction against the governing body.

f. Public education as carried out by an ethical psychiatrist would not utilize appeals based solely upon emotion, but would be presented in a professional way and without any potential exploitation of patients through testimonials.

4. A psychiatrist should not be a participant in a legally authorized execution.

SECTION 2

A physician shall deal honestly with patients and colleagues, and strive to expose those physicians deficient in character or competence, or who engage in fraud or deception.

1. The requirement that the physician conduct himself with propriety in his/her profession and in all the actions of his/her life is especially important in the case of the psychiatrist because the patient tends to model his/her behavior after that of his/her therapist by identification. Further, the necessary intensity of the therapeutic relationship may tend to activate sexual and other needs and fantasies on the part of both patient and therapist, while weakening the objectivity necessary for control. Sexual activity with a patient is unethical.

2. The psychiatrist should diligently guard against exploiting information furnished by the patient and should not use the unique position of power afforded him/her by the psychotherapeutic situation to influence the patient in any way not directly relevant to the treatment goals.

3. A psychiatrist who regularly practices outside his/her area of professional competence should be considered unethical. Determination of professional competence should be made by peer review boards or other appropriate bodies.

4. Special consideration should be given to those psychiatrists who, because of mental illness, jeopardize the welfare of their patients and their own reputations and practices. It is ethical, even encouraged, for another psychiatrist to intercede in such situations.

5. Psychiatric services, like all medical services, are dispensed in the context of a contractual arrangement between the patient and the treating physician. The provisions of the contractual arrangement, which are binding on the physician as well as on the patient, should be explicitly established.

6. It is ethical for the psychiatrist to make a charge for a missed appointment when this falls within the terms of the specific contractual agreement with the patient. Charging for a missed appointment or for one not cancelled 24 hours in advance need not, in itself, be considered unethical if a patient is fully advised that the physician will make such a charge. The practice, however, should be resorted to infrequently and always with the utmost consideration of the patient and his/her circumstances.

7. An arrangement in which a psychiatrist provides supervision or administration to other physicians or nonmedical persons for a percentage of their fees or gross income is not acceptable; this would constitute fee-splitting. In a team of practitioners, or a multidisciplinary team, it is ethical for the psychiatrist to receive income for administration, research, education, or consultation. This should be based upon a mutually agreed upon and set fee or salary, open to renegotiation when a change in the time demand occurs. (See also Section 5, Annotations 2, 3, and 4.)

8. When a member has been found to have behaved unethically by the American Psychiatric Association or one of its constituent district branches, there should not be automatic reporting to the local authorities responsible for medical licensure, but the decision to report should be decided upon the merits of the case.

SECTION 3

A physician shall respect the law and also recognize a responsibility to seek changes in those requirements which are contrary to the best interests of the patient.

1. It would seem self-evident that a psychiatrist who is a law-breaker might be ethically unsuited to practice his/her profession. When such illegal activities bear directly upon his/her practice, this would obviously be the case. However, in other instances, illegal activities such as those concerning the right to protest social injustices might not bear on either the image of the psychiatrist or the ability of the specific psychiatrist to treat his/her patient ethically and well. While no committee or board could offer prior assurance that any illegal activity would not be considered unethical, it is conceivable that an individual could violate a law without being guilty of professionally unethical behavior. Physicians lose no right of citizenship on entry into the profession of medicine.

2. Where not specifically prohibited by local laws governing medical practice, the practice of acupuncture by a psychiatrist is not unethical per se. The psychiatrist should have professional competence in the use of acupuncture. Or, if he/she is supervising the use of acupuncture by nonmedical individuals, he/she should provide proper medical supervision. (See also Section 5, Annotations 3 and 4.)

SECTION 4

A physician shall respect the rights of patients, of colleagues, and of other health professionals, and shall safeguard patient confidences within the constraints of the law.

1. Psychiatric records, including even the identification of a person as a patient, must be protected with extreme care. Confidentiality is essential to psychiatric treatment. This is based in part on the special nature of psychiatric therapy as well as on the traditional ethical relationship between physician and patient. Growing con-

cern regarding the civil rights of patients and the possible adverse effects of computerization, duplication equipment, and data banks makes the dissemination of confidential information an increasing hazard. Because of the sensitive and private nature of the information with which the psychiatrist deals, he/she must be circumspect in the information that he/she chooses to disclose to others about a patient. The welfare of the patient must be a continuing consideration.

2. A psychiatrist may release confidential information only with the authorization of the patient or under proper legal compulsion. The continuing duty of the psychiatrist to protect the patient includes fully apprising him/her of the connotations of waiving the privilege of privacy. This may become an issue when the patient is being investigated by a government agency, is applying for a position, or is involved in legal action. The same principles apply to the release of information concerning treatment to medical departments of government agencies, business organizations, labor unions, and insurance companies. Information gained in confidence about patients seen in student health services should not be released without the student's explicit permission.

3. Clinical and other materials used in teaching and writing must be adequately disguised in order to preserve the anonymity of the individuals involved.

4. The ethical responsibility of maintaining confidentiality holds equally for the consultations in which the patient may not have been present and in which the consultee was not a physician. In such instances, the physician consultant should alert the consultee to his/her duty of confidentiality.

5. Ethically the psychiatrist may disclose only that information which is relevant to a given situation. He/she should avoid offering speculation as fact. Sensitive information such as an individual's sexual orientation or fantasy material is usually unnecessary.

6. Psychiatrists are often asked to examine individuals for security purposes, to determine suitability for various jobs, and to determine legal competence. The psychiatrist must fully describe the nature and purpose and lack of confidentiality of the examination to the examinee at the beginning of the examination.

7. Careful judgment must be exercised by the psychiatrist in order to include, when appropriate, the parents or guardian in the treatment of a minor. At the same time the psychiatrist must assure the minor proper confidentiality.

8. Psychiatrists at times may find it necessary, in order to protect the patient or the community from imminent danger, to reveal confidential information disclosed by the patient.

9. When the psychiatrist is ordered by the court to reveal the confidences entrusted to him/her by patients he/she may comply or he/she may ethically hold the right to dissent within the framework of the law. When the psychiatrist is in doubt, the right of the patient to confidentiality and, by extension, to unimpaired treatment,

should be given priority. The psychiatrist should reserve the right to raise the question of adequate need for disclosure. In the event that the necessity for legal disclosure is demonstrated by the court, the psychiatrist may request the right to disclosure of only that information which is relevant to the legal question at hand.

10. With regard for the person's dignity and privacy and with truly informed consent, it is ethical to present a patient to a scientific gathering, if the confidentiality of the presentation is understood and accepted by the audience.

11. It is ethical to present a patient or former patient to a public gathering or to the news media only if that patient is fully informed of enduring loss of confidentiality, is competent, and consents in writing without coercion.

12. When involved in funded research, the ethical psychiatrist will advise human subjects of the funding source, retain his/her freedom to reveal data and results, and follow all appropriate and current guidelines relative to human subject protection.

13. Ethical considerations in medical practice preclude the psychiatric evaluation of any adult charged with criminal acts prior to access to, or availability of, legal counsel. The only exception is the rendering of care to the person for the sole purpose of medical treatment.

SECTION 5

A physician shall continue to study, apply, and advance scientific knowledge, make relevant information available to patients, colleagues, and the public, obtain consultation, and use the talents of other health professionals when indicated.

1. Psychiatrists are responsible for their own continuing education and should be mindful of the fact that theirs must be a lifetime of learning.

2. In the practice of his/her specialty, the psychiatrist consults, associates, collaborates, or integrates his/her work with that of many professionals, including psychologists, psychometricians, social workers, alcoholism counselors, marriage counselors, public health nurses, etc. Furthermore, the nature of modern psychiatric practice extends his/her contacts to such people as teachers, juvenile and adult probation officers, attorneys, welfare workers, agency volunteers, and neighborhood aides. In referring patients for treatment, counseling, or rehabilitation to any of these practitioners, the psychiatrist should ensure that the allied professional or paraprofessional with whom he/she is dealing is a recognized member of his/her own discipline and is competent to carry out the therapeutic task required. The psychiatrist should have the same attitude toward members of the medical profession to whom he/she refers patients. Whenever he/she has reason to doubt the training, skill, or ethical qualifications of the allied professional, the psychiatrist should not refer cases to him/her.

3. When the psychiatrist assumes a collaborative or supervisory role with another mental health worker, he/she must expend sufficient time to assure that proper care is given. It is contrary to the interests of the patient and to patient care if he/she allows himself/herself to be used as a figurehead.

4. In relationships between psychiatrists and practicing licensed psychologists, the physician should not delegate to the psychologist or, in fact, to any nonmedical person any matter requiring the exercise of professional medical judgment.

5. The psychiatrist should agree to the request of a patient for consultation or to such a request from the family of an incompetent or minor patient. The psychiatrist may suggest possible consultants, but the patient or family should be given free choice of the consultant. If the psychiatrist disapproves of the professional qualifications of the consultant or if there is a difference of opinion that the primary therapist cannot resolve, he/she may, after suitable notice, withdraw from the case. If this disagreement occurs within an institution or agency framework, the differences should be resolved by the mediation or arbitration of higher professional authority within the institution or agency.

SECTION 6

A physician shall, in the provision of appropriate patient care, except in emergencies, be free to choose whom to serve, with whom to associate, and the environment in which to provide medical services.

1. Physicians generally agree that the doctor-patient relationship is such a vital factor in effective treatment of the patient that preservation of optimal conditions for development of a sound working relationship between a doctor and his/her patient should take precedence over all other considerations. Professional courtesy may lead to poor psychiatric care for physicians and their families because of embarrassment over the lack of a complete give-and-take contract.

2. An ethical psychiatrist may refuse to provide psychiatric treatment to a person who, in the psychiatrist's opinion, cannot be diagnosed as having a mental illness amenable to psychiatric treatment.

SECTION 7

A physician shall recognize a responsibility to participate in activities contributing to an improved community.

1. Psychiatrists should foster the cooperation of those legitimately concerned with the medical, psychological, social, and legal aspects of mental health and illness. Psychiatrists are encouraged to serve society by advising and consulting with the executive, legislative, and judiciary branches of the government. A psychiatrist should clarify whether he/she speaks as an individual or as a representative of an organization. Furthermore, psychiatrists should avoid cloaking their public statements with the authority of the profession (e.g., "Psychiatrists know that . . .").

2. Psychiatrists may interpret and share with the public their expertise in the various psychosocial issues that may affect mental health and illness. Psychiatrists should always be mindful of their separate roles as dedicated citizens and as experts in psychological medicine.

3. On occasion psychiatrists are asked for an opinion about an individual who is in the light of public attention, or who has disclosed information about himself/herself through public media. It is unethical for a psychiatrist to offer a professional opinion unless he/she has conducted an examination and has been granted proper authorization for such a statement.

4. The psychiatrist may permit his/her certification to be used for the involuntary treatment of any person only following his/her personal examination of that person. To do so, he/she must find that the person, because of mental illness, cannot form a judgment as to what is in his/her own best interests and that, without such treatment, substantial impairment is likely to occur to the person or others.

Procedures for Handling Complaints of Unethical Conduct[5]

A complaint concerning the behavior of a member of this Association shall be in writing, signed by the complainant, and filed with the Secretary. The Secretary shall refer it to the appropriate District Branch for investigation and action. The Secretary shall notify the accused member of the receipt of such a complaint and that it has been forwarded to the member's local District Branch and shall inform the accused member of his or her right to appeal any forthcoming action to the Board. The District Branch may appeal to the Board for relief from responsibility for considering any complaint. The member against whom the complaint was brought shall have the right of appeal to the Board for reconsideration of the decision of the District Branch.[6]

As noted above, a complaint must be written, must be signed by the complainant, and must be filed with the Secretary of the Association.

Procedure A. Allegation Received by District Branch

I.   District Branch:

   A. Receives signed communication alleging or inferring unethical conduct.

   B. Determines the membership status of the potential defendant.

   C. Determines if allegation or inference constitutes a complaint of unethical conduct as defined in the PRINCIPLES OF MEDICAL ETHICS WITH ANNOTATIONS ESPECIALLY APPLICABLE TO PSYCHIATRY — that is, does the allegation or inference merit an investigation—and, if so, files a copy of the complaint with the Secretary of the American Psychiatric Association.

II. Secretary of the American Psychiatric Association:

   A. Receives written and signed copy of the complaint from the District Branch and refers complaint back to the Branch for investigation.

   B. Notifies the accused member that a copy of a complaint has been received and filed, that the investigation will be conducted by the District Branch, and of the member's right to appeal a negative decision to the Board of Trustees of the American Psychiatric Association.

---

[5]Approved by the Executive Committee and the Assembly, 1975; revision approved by the Board of Trustees and the Assembly, 1977.

[6]Chapter 10, Section 1, By-Laws, American Psychiatric Association, 1981 revision.

III. District Branch:

   A. Upon receiving complaint from the Secretary of the American Psychiatric Association, notifies the accused member of the complaint, who made the complaint, relates the complaint to the appropriate Section(s) of the PRINCIPLES OF MEDICAL ETHICS WITH ANNOTATIONS ESPECIALLY APPLICABLE TO PSYCHIATRY, informs the accused member of his/her right to be advised and represented by legal counsel, and forward to him/her a copy of the complaint, these PROCEDURES, the PRINCIPLES OF MEDICAL ETHICS WITH ANNOTATIONS ESPECIALLY APPLICABLE TO PSYCHIATRY, all addenda to the PROCEDURES and PRINCIPLES, and a copy of the Constitution and By-Laws of the American Psychiatric Association.

   B. Notifies complainant that the complaint has been received and will be investigated, of his/her right to legal counsel during the investigation, and that he/she will be informed of the decision of the District Branch.

   C. Refers the complaint to the District Branch Ethics Committee or whatever body serves that function for investigation and recommendations for action to the Council of the District Branch.

   D. Ethics Committee or whatever body serves that function investigates the complaint, permitting both the defendant and complainant to be heard. If the complainant is expected to produce evidence, he/she should be so advised in writing.

   E. May refer the complaint to the American Psychiatric Association for investigation under unusual circumstances and then PROCEDURE B would be followed, with the APA Ethics Committee conducting the investigation. Unusual circumstances would include, but not be limited to, conflicts of interest, interested parties from different parts of the country, or a complaint of significant national importance.

   F. The Council of the District Branch, upon receiving the recommendation for action, determines:

      1. Either that the complaint is without merit and dismisses it;

      2. Or, that the complaint has been sustained and the defendant shall be subject to one of the following penalties:

         a. admonishment
         b. reprimand

      c. suspension from membership for a specific period of time
      d. expulsion from the District Branch.

  G. Notifies the Secretary of the American Psychiatric Association of the procedures followed, the Section under which the complaint was filed, and the action taken.

IV.   Secretary of the American Psychiatric Association:

  A. Receives the report of the District Branch.

  B. Sends the report to the Ethics Committee of the American Psychiatric Association.

V.   Ethics Committee of the American Psychiatric Association:

  A. Reviews the procedures followed by the District Branch.

  B. Obtains additional information from the District Branch about procedures if necessary.

  C. Reports to the Board of Trustees on the procedures followed and the action taken.

VI.   Board of Trustees of the American Psychiatric Association:

  A. On recommendation of the Ethics Committee of the American Psychiatric Association:

    1. Approves that proper procedures have been followed. If not approved, the District Branch is directed to complete this investigation properly following the procedures.

    2. Receives the report of action taken.

    3. Orders the action taken be kept in a confidential file, listed by initial of the defendant only.

    4. When expulsion from the District Branch is the action, notifies the defendant of his expulsion from the American Psychiatric Association and his right of appeal.

  B. Instructs the Secretary of the American Psychiatric Association to notify the District Branch whether or not proper procedures have been followed.

VII. District Branch:

  A. Notifies the accused member of action taken and his/her rights of appeal.

  B. Notifies complainant of action taken after avenues of appeal to the American Psychiatric Association have been exhausted or waived.

VIII. Appeal Procedure:

    A. Within thirty (30) days of receipt of notice of action by the District Branch (and the Board of Trustees in case of expulsion), the defendant files written notice of his/her appeal with the Secretary of the American Psychiatric Association.

    B. The Secretary of the American Psychiatric Association notifies the District Branch of the appeal and asks them to submit all information in their possession. The defendant is asked to submit the justification for his/her appeal and any information which he/she has which would support his/her appeal.

    C. This information is submitted to the APA Ethics Committee. The defendant, with thirty (30) days' written notice, has the right to personal appearance, accompanied by legal counsel if he/she wishes, before the APA Ethics Committee. The APA Ethics Committee has the right to request the defendant and/or complainant to appear, with legal counsel if desired by either. (See Procedure B.IV.D.)

Procedure B. Allegation Received by the American Psychiatric Association

I.   Secretary of the American Psychiatric Association:

    A. Receives signed communication alleging or inferring unethical conduct.

    B. Determines the membership status of the potential defendant.

    C. Determines if allegation or inference constitutes a complaint of unethical conduct as defined in the PRINCIPLES OF MEDICAL ETHICS WITH ANNOTATIONS ESPECIALLY APPLICABLE TO PSYCHIATRY — that is, does the allegation or inference merit an investigation.

    D. Notifies the accused member of the complaint, who made the complaint, relates the complaint to the appropriate Section(s) of the PRINCIPLES OF MEDICAL ETHICS WITH ANNOTATIONS ESPECIALLY APPLICABLE TO PSYCHIATRY, informs the accused member of his/her right to be advised and represented by legal counsel, and forwards to him/her a copy of the complaint, these PROCEDURES, the PRINCIPLES OF MEDICAL ETHICS WITH ANNOTATIONS ESPECIALLY APPLICABLE TO PSYCHIATRY, all addenda to the PROCEDURES and PRINCIPLES, and a copy of the Constitution and By-Laws of the American Psychiatric Association.

    E. Notifies complainant that complaint has been received, that an investigation will be conducted by the District

Branch (or APA Ethics Committee), advises him/her of his/her right to legal counsel during the investigation, and that he/she will be informed of the decision.

F. Sends complaint to the District Branch for investigation with information to the APA Ethics Committee.

II. District Branch:

A. Accepts the responsibility and assigns investigation to its Ethics Committee or whatever body acts in that capacity (and the Committee follows Procedure A.I); recommendations from that body are made to the Council of the District Branch.

B. The Council of the District Branch determines:

1. Either that the complaint is without merit and dismisses it;

2. Or, that the complaint has been sustained and the defendant shall be subject to one of the following penalties:

   a. admonishment
   b. reprimand
   c. suspension from membership for a specific period of time
   d. expulsion from the District Branch.

C. The Council of the District Branch notifies the Secretary of the American Psychiatric Association of the procedures followed and the action recommended.

III. Secretary of the American Psychiatric Association:

A. Reviews the procedures and recommendations of the District Branch.

B. Sends the report to the APA Ethics Committee.

IV. Ethics Committee of the American Psychiatric Association:

A. Reviews the procedures and recommendations of the District Branch.

B. Obtains additional information from the District Branch about procedures and recommendations if necessary.

C. Reports to the APA Board of Trustees on the procedures followed and actions recommended.

D. When the APA Ethics Committee is the original investigating body:

1. The Ethics Committee may request two Fellows of the American Psychiatric Association residing in the same area as the complainant and defendant to serve as in-

vestigators. These investigators may interview the parties and gather other pertinent information, which they will submit to the Ethics Committee. If the complainant is expected to produce evidence, he/she should be so advised in writing.

2. Because of possible distances involved, the defendant and complainant shall be given thirty (30) days' notice in writing of the time and place of the meeting of the Ethics Committee.

3. The defendant and complainant shall have the right to appear and to legal counsel.

4. The Ethics Committee makes its recommendation to the Board of Trustees.

V. Board of Trustees of the American Psychiatric Association:

A. On recommendation of the APA Ethics Committee:

1. Approves that proper procedures have been followed. If not approved, the District Branch (or the Ethics Committee if the investigating body) is directed to complete their investigation properly following the procedures.

2. Approves, disapproves, or modifies the action recommended by the District Branch (or the Ethics Committee if the investigating body). In case of expulsion, a two-thirds (2/3) vote of the Board of Trustees is required.

3. Notifies the complainant after avenues of appeal have been exhausted or waived, and the defendant and the District Branch of the action taken. The defendant is again advised of his/her right to appeal and to be represented by legal counsel.

4. Orders the action taken be kept in a confidential file, listed by initial of the defendant only.

5. In the case of expulsion, the member is also expelled from the District Branch.

VI. Appeal Procedure:

A. Within thirty (30) days of receipt of notice of action by the APA Board of Trustees, the defendant files written notice with the Secretary of the American Psychiatric Association of his/her appeal.

B. Expelled members shall be denied all membership privileges pending the appeal.

C. All other penalties shall be suspended pending the appeal.

D. The appeal shall be heard at the next Annual Meeting of the American Psychiatric Association at a session attended only by voting members and the necessary secretarial staff and legal counsel as selected by the President.

E. The defendant shall have the right to be heard, present his/her evidence, and be represented by legal counsel.

F. Presentation of evidence and arguments for the American Psychiatric Association shall be made by the President or a member of his choice.

G. A two-thirds (2/3) vote of those present by secret written ballot shall be required to reverse the action of the Board of Trustees, leading to a modified action or dismissal of the charges.

Outline of District Branch Report to the American Psychiatric Association (After Investigation)

Dear Secretary:

We have concluded our investigation into the ethical complaint filed against Dr. _____ about which we previously notified you on _____ . The following procedures were followed:

	Yes	No

1. The accused member was interviewed by our ethics committee or other investigating body.
2. The accused member was represented by counsel.
3. The accused member called witnesses on his/her behalf.
4. The accused member introduced other evidence on his/her behalf.
5. The complainant or his/her legal counsel questioned the accused member and/or other witnesses.
6. The complainant was interviewed by our ethics committee or other investigating body.
7. The complainant was represented by counsel.
8. The complainant called witnesses on his/her behalf.
9. The complainant introduced other evidence on his/her behalf.
10. The accused member and/or his/her counsel questioned the complainant and other witnesses.

Describe any other procedures followed: _____

On the basis of our investigation, we have found the accused member in violation of the Principles of Medical Ethics with Annotations Especially Applicable to Psychiatry, Section _____. Our basis for this conclusion is as follows:

(Here the District Branch should include a brief statement—1/2 to 1 page—of the reasons for its decision; e.g., accused member admitted, complainant's allegations did not withstand questioning, documentary evidence, etc.)

We believe that the accused member should be (admonished, reprimanded, suspended [for _____ years], expelled). Our basis for this sanction is as follows:

(Here the District Branch should give a brief statement—1/4 to 1/2 page—of its reasons for the sanction; e.g., very serious offense, accused member in treatment, not likely to repeat, etc.)

Suggested District Branch Letter to the Accused Member (Before Investigation)

Dear Dr. _____ :

This is to notify you that an ethical complaint against you has been filed by _____. A copy of the complaint is enclosed. The complaint alleges violations of the Principles of Medical Ethics with Annotations Especially Applicable to Psychiatry, Section _____. This district branch will be investigating the complaint. You are advised that you have the right to be represented by legal counsel during these proceedings. We will notify you as the investigation proceeds.

We are enclosing a copy of the Constitution and By-Laws of the American Psychiatric Association, as well as a copy of the Procedures for Handling Complaints of Unethical Conduct and the Principles of Medical Ethics with Annotations Especially Applicable to Psychiatry.

If you have any questions, please write to this district branch.

Very truly yours,

Suggested District Branch Letter to Complainant (Before Investigation)

Dear _____:

This is to notify you that this district branch of the American Psychiatric Association will be investigating the ethics complaint you have filed against Dr. _____. You will be advised of the information that will be requested from you as the investigation proceeds. You are entitled to be represented by legal counsel with respect to these proceedings.

While every effort will be made to proceed expeditiously, the seriousness of this matter requires that we proceed carefully. In addition, the process contemplates possible appeals to the American Psychiatric Association as well, and therefore may take a considerable period of time before final resolution. You will be notified of the outcome at that time.

Very truly yours,